MAKING MINIATURE FURNITURE

Richard A. Lyons
and
Elizabeth G. Lyons

DOVER PUBLICATIONS, INC.
Mineola, New York

*We wish to dedicate this book to our children, Elizabeth
Andrea, and Richard. We wish to thank you for being such
fine adults – even though it seems only yesterday that you
were 4 and 3.*

Bibliographical Note

This Dover edition, first published in 1999, is an unabridged republi-
cation of the work originally published by Prentice-Hall, Inc., Englewood
Cliffs, New Jersey, in 1988.

Library of Congress Cataloging-in-Publication Data

Lyons, Richard A.
  Making miniature furniture / Richard A. Lyons and Elizabeth G.
Lyons.
      p. cm.
  Originally published: Englewood Cliffs, N.J. : Prentice-Hall, c1988.
  ISBN 0-486-40719-5 (pbk.)
    1. Miniature furniture. I. Lyons, Elizabeth G. II. Title.
TT178 .L96 1999
684.1'00228—dc21

                                                                99-048937

Manufactured in the United States of America
Dover Publications, Inc., 31 East 2nd Street, Mineola, N.Y. 11501

Contents

Preface

Artifacts of our oldest cultures give evidence that the human race has always made things in miniature. The early American Indians made dolls, toys, and miniature implements for their children. Toys have been found in the Egyptian tombs as well as in archaeological digs of ancient China. The fascination for things in miniature is still strong for most people today. What we do not realize, in most instances, is what size reduction does to an object. As an example, Plate 1 shows a full-size candle stand that has been brought to one-half scale and to one-fourth scale. When reducing an item by scale, every measurement is reduced. This compounds the effect of the scaling-down process.

It is important to realize that miniaturizing a piece requires more accuracy in the work. When working with $\frac{1}{2}$-in.-thick stock rather than 1-in. stock, a $\frac{1}{32}$-in. error represents a larger percentage of the total thickness of the $\frac{1}{2}$-in. stock than it does for the 1-in. stock. Since most antique furniture is made with $\frac{7}{8}$-in.-thick stock, half-scale reduction would require the use of $\frac{7}{16}$in.-thick stock. From the standpoint of strength and durability, I have found that $\frac{7}{16}$-in.-thick stock makes the work fragile and is not practical if children are to play with the pieces. Therefore, I have used $\frac{1}{2}$-in. stock in most of the pieces presented in this book. This extra $\frac{1}{16}$ of an inch of thickness does not adversely affect the style or proportions of the pieces. To use $\frac{3}{4}$-in.-thick stock for the work would result in a bulky, out-of-proportion piece. The one exception is the settle in Chapter 6. Since this piece is large enough for a child to sit in, I felt that it would be wise to make it rather strong.

For your work to have excellent style and proportion you will need some way to reduce your stock to the $\frac{1}{2}$-in. thickness. If you have the good fortune to have access to a planer, this will be no problem. I was not that fortunate and was required to drive far and pay handsomely to have planer work done. Recently, I was able to afford the surfacer

Plate 1   Affects of Scaling Down

Plate 2   Wilke 13-in. Surfacer

shown in Plate 2. It is of high quality and affordable, and is available through the Wilke Machinery Works of York, Pennsylvania.

The dolls used in illustrating the pieces of furniture are antique dolls that Elizabeth has collected. The size and type of doll used in the settings is given.

My sources for good-quality miniature hardware and special tools were the following:

Ball and Ball Company
463 W. Lincoln Highway
Exton, PA 19341
(610) 363-7330

Woodcraft Supply Corporation
313 Montvale Avenue
Woburn, MA 01801
(781) 935-6414

Wilke Machinery Works
3230 Susquehanna Trail
York, PA 17402
(717) 764-5000

About the Authors

The Lyons have been collecting antique dolls, toys, and furniture for over 30 years. Their saltbox style home located in West Central Indiana holds many treasures found as a result of their searches. Nestled among full size pieces of antique furniture, can be found many miniature works with one or more of Elizabeth's antique dolls near by.

Richard's well-equipped woodworking shop, and Elizabeth's skills with doll repairs, makes it a pleasure to find and restore antique furniture and antique dolls.

Richard is a professor, and Chairman of the Department of Electronics and Computer Technology at Indiana State University, and Elizabeth is a home maker, and avid member of the local doll clubs.

Making Miniature Furniture is the third book in a series on furniture by Richard Lyons. The earlier books are *Identifying and Repairing Antique Furniture* and *Making Country Furniture.*

Chapter 1

Construction Concepts

In this chapter we discuss and illustrate some of the basic concepts of furniture construction. We will refer throughout to the material covered in this chapter.

GROOVED JOINTS

Grooved joints have a groove or recess cut into one member of the work, either along the grain or across the grain, into which the edge, end, or entire part of another member of the work will fit. Figure 1-1 shows a groove that has been cut into the edge of a piece of stock. The groove is used to hold panels in frames such as paneled doors and paneled ends on chests of drawers. It is normal for the groove to be set in the center of the edge, deep enough for the panel member to expand without binding and to contract without creating a crack.

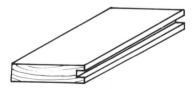

Figure 1-1   Groove Joint

Figure 1-2 shows a rabbet joint. When cut on the inside rear corner of a cupboard or chest, a rabbet joint provides a shoulder on which to fasten a back. The rabbet joint usually comes in from the face about one-half the thickness of the stock in which the joint is cut, with a depth equal to the thickness of the stock it is to support. A rabbet joint may also be used in drawer construction, as will be shown later.

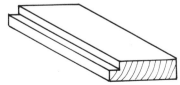

Figure 1-2   Rabbet Joint

Figure 1-3 shows a dado joint. The dado joint is a groove cut across the grain. This joint is used on shelves, bookcases, and cabinets, and to secure the back of a drawer to the side of a drawer. A dado that does not go all the way across the stock is referred to as a gain joint or stopped dado. The gain joint is used at the front edge of a desk or any fine piece of furniture to hide the dado joint. A gain joint is shown in Figure 1-4.

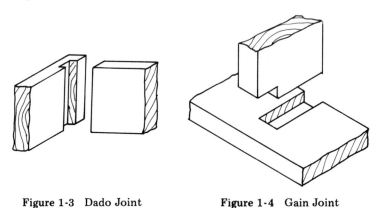

Figure 1-3   Dado Joint   Figure 1-4   Gain Joint

LAP JOINTS

To form a lap joint, half the thickness of each member is cut away, then the members are joined. The resulting surfaces are flush. Figure 1-5 shows an end lap joint, and Figure 1-6 shows a cross lap joint. Lap

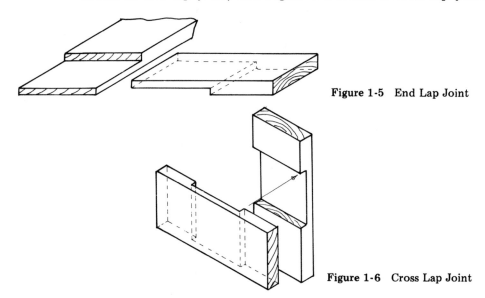

Figure 1-5   End Lap Joint

Figure 1-6   Cross Lap Joint

joints are often placed on the edges of stock of random width to form a back for a hutch, settle, or any piece of such width that a single board is not practical. This use of the edge lap joint is used on the cabinets featured in Chapter 5.

A much stronger lap joint, the dovetail lap joint, is shown in Figure 1-7. The dovetail is formed and half of the thickness of the stock is removed. A mortise is then cut half the thickness into the second member. When the two members are joined, the surface is flush.

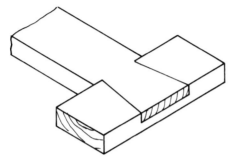

Figure 1-7   Dovetail Lap Joint

A slightly different application of the dovetail lap joint is shown in Figure 1-8. This style of dovetail lap joint is often used to join the top stretcher of a chest of drawers to the post.

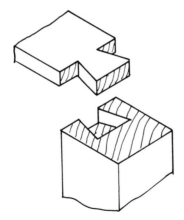

Figure 1-8   Dovetail Lap Joint

MORTISE-AND-TENON JOINTS

Probably the strongest and most desirable joint that can be used when building up the carcass of a piece of furniture is the hidden mortise-and-tenon joint with a pin inserted. Figure 1-9 shows a mortise-and-tenon joint. There is no set rule concerning the thickness of the tenon, but it should be thick enough to give strength, but not so thick that there is danger of the mortise breaking out of the face of the mortised member. With the exception of the bareface tenon joint, the tenon is placed in the center of the member. If the mortise is to be placed near the end of a piece of stock, the shoulder should be cut down at least ½ in. to avoid splitting out the end grain.

Figure 1-10 shows the bareface mortise and tenon. This joint is used when rails and legs of stools or tables are to be made flush. Occasionally, a bareface tenon will be used when the mortise member is very small in thickness or cross section.

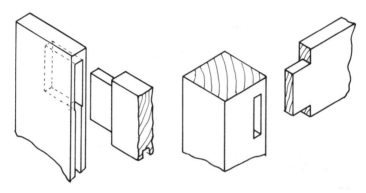

Figure 1-9   Mortise
and Tenon Joint

Figure 1-10   Bareface
Mortise and Tenon Joint

Figure 1-11a and b show the use of the dovetail as a type of mortising joint. Figure 1-11a illustrates the dovetail as a through multiple dovetail joint used for bracket feet and base moldings on fine furniture. Figure 1-11b shows the use of the dovetail as a half-lap multiple dovetail joint used to secure drawer sides to drawer fronts.

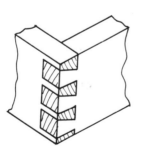

Figure 1-11a   Through
Multiple Dovetail Joint

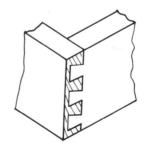

Figure 1-11b   Half-lap
Multiple Dovetail Joint

DRAWER CONSTRUCTION

There are three basic ways to construct drawers, each appropriate to a certain style of furniture.

Box Style of Drawer Construction

Figure 1-12 illustrates the most primitive type of drawer construction. This is nothing more than a box with a false front added, and belongs on only the most primitive work. Notice that the bottom is nailed to the bottom edges of the sides and back. In some cases the bottom fits up into the box and is secured with nails driven through the sides, front, and back.

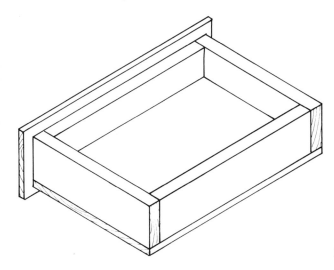

Figure 1-12   Box Style
Drawer Construction

Dado Style of Drawer Construction

This type of drawer construction is shown in Figure 1-13. It makes use of the dado joint, the groove, and the rabbet joint. The bottom sets up into a groove that has been cut on the inside face of the front and sides, and fits under the back of the drawer. In this type of drawer construction the first step is always to select the stock for the drawer front and cut to fit in the opening with approximately $\frac{1}{32}$ in. of clearance. The length of the sides should be such that the drawer, when closed, will fit flush with the front of the work. The groove that holds the bottom should not have a depth more than half the thickness of the stock for the side, and the groove should be approximately ½ in. up from the bottom edge. The rabbet cut across the grain of the front should be wide enough for the sides to fit flush with the ends of the drawer front, and have a depth of about three-fourths of the thickness of the stock used for the front. This style of construction is quite acceptable for primitive- and country-style furniture.

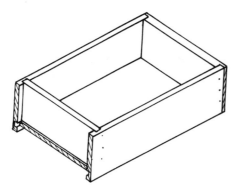

Figure 1-13   Dado Style Drawer Construction

Dovetail Construction of Drawers

Without a doubt, drawers constructed using dovetails are both the most demanding in terms of skill and the most desirable. Dovetail drawer construction is the only type that is permissible in fine classical period furniture. Although the dovetail joints used in the construction of the slope-top desk illustrated in Chapter 7 could be replaced by a dado joint, the overall quality of the work would suffer. Figure 1-14 illustrates a typical drawer constructed with a dovetail.

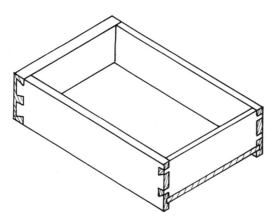

Figure 1-14   Dovetail Style of Drawer Construction

Notice that the dovetail is similar to the dadoed drawer shown in Figure 1-13, except that dovetails are used throughout. For drawer construction the dovetails do not have to be uniform in width. However, the length of the dovetails should be about three-fourths of the thickness of the drawer front. As always, the first step in constructing the drawer is cutting the drawer front to fit the opening with $\frac{1}{32}$ in. of clearance. Second, the groove that is cut in the inside face of the sides and front to hold the bottom should be placed so that it aligns with the center of the bottom dovetail. This will completely hide the groove when the drawer is assembled. The back of the drawer will be the same length as the front of the drawer.

LATCHES

In the past, hardware for furniture was not readily available to the cabinetmaker who lived inland from the large seaport population centers. To overcome this problem, hinges were hammered out by the local blacksmith, and the cabinetmaker carved his own style of fasteners for doors. Figure 1-15 illustrates how a keeper and turnbuckle are used to hold a pair of doors in place. The keeper is fastened to the inside surface of one door, and fits into a notch cut into a shelf or behind a stile. The turnbuckle is mounted on the companion door with a knob exposed on the outside. When turned, the flange of the turnbuckle would pass behind a face board or a companion door and hold in place the door to which it was attached. The two doors in Figure 15a meet with an edge half-lap joint. This is not necessary but does make a nice tight cabinet. The keeper and flange on the turnbuckle were usually carved or whittled to shape, and the knob and shaft were turned on a lathe.

The small hinges and hardware can be obtained from the Ball and Ball Company. The complete address is given in the Introduction.

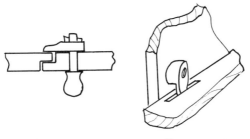

Figure 1-15a
Turnbuckle

Figure 1-15b
Door Keeper

Chapter 2

Tables

STAND TABLES

Small tables have many uses in the home. The one shown is constructed using mortise-and-tenon joints to fasten the rails to the legs. The top is secured with screws brought through holes bored at an angle on the inside surface of the rails. This feature is shown in Figure 2-1.

Bill of Materials

Number required	Part name and number	Size (in.)				
		T	×	W	×	L
4	Leg (1)	1		1		9½
4	Rail (2)	½		1½		6
1	Top (3)	½		9		9

STEPS OF PROCEDURE

1. Select the stock for the legs, and lay out and cut the mortises as shown in Figure 2-1.
2. Select the stock for the rails, and lay out and cut the tenons as shown in Figure 2-1.
3. Trial-fit the tenons to the mortises.
4. Cut the taper on the legs as illustrated in the front and side views.
5. Select the stock for the top and cut to the correct size.
6. Permanently assemble the legs and rails with glue.
7. Secure the top to the frame of legs with screws as shown in Figure 2-1.

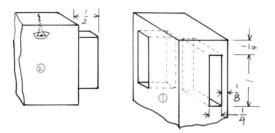

Figure 2-1

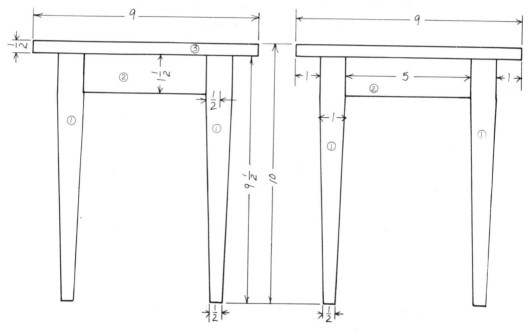

Stand Table

HUTCH TABLE

The hutch table is a dual-purpose device. When the top is down, it can be used as a worktable or eating table. With the top tilted vertically, the piece can be placed against the wall to provide a place to set small items. The woman shown is preparing the table for serving a meal.

Plate 4   Hutch table. Doll: 25-in. china head.

Bill of Materials

Number required	Name of part and number	Size (in.)		
		T × W	×	L
2	End (1)	½	6	14½
2	Side (2)	½	5¼	9½
2	Foot (3)	1	1½	12
1	Stretcher (4)	½	1½	9
2	Brace (5)	½	1	18
1	Shelf (6)	½	6	8½
1	Top (7)	½	18	18

STEPS OF PROCEDURE

1. Select the stock for the ends, and lay out and cut the tenons that are to fit into the feet.
2. Lay out the design on the bottom of the ends, and cut as shown on the end view.

3. Select the stock for the sides, and cut the dovetails on the ends as shown on the front view.

4. Locate the position for the mortises on the edges of ends, and using the dovetails cut in the sides as a pattern, cut the mortises to fit individual dovetails. Be sure to mark which dovetail goes with which mortise.

5. Select the stock for the feet, and cut to the correct size.

6. Lay out the mortises that are to receive the tenons on the bottom of the ends.

7. Chisel out the mortises, and individually fit to the tenons. Be sure to mark which tenon goes to which mortise.

8. Select the stock for the stretcher, and cut to the correct size.

9. Cut dovetails on the ends of the stretcher as shown in Figure 2-2.

10. Trial-fit the feet to the ends, and trial-fit the sides to the ends.

11. With the ends, sides, and feet trial-assembled, place the stretcher in the proper position.

12. Using as patterns the dovetails that are cut on the stretcher, lay out the mortises for the dovetails in the center of the feet (see Figure 2-2).

13. Remove the feet from the ends, and cut the mortises for the dovetails on the stretcher.

14. Trial-assemble the table, placing the feet, sides, stretcher, and ends together.

15. Select the stock for the shelf and fit on top of the braces.

16. Select the stock for the top and cut to size.

17. Select the stock for the braces and cut to size. Shape as shown in the end view.

18. Secure the braces to the bottom surface of the top.

19. Temporarily place the top on the base of the table and determine exactly where the pivot holes are to be drilled. (Even though the positions of the holes are shown on the drawing, follow step 19 to be sure that there is no major difference between your work and the plans.)

20. Remove the top and drill four $\frac{1}{2}$-in. holes in the braces.

21. Place the top on the base in the proper position and mark where $\frac{1}{2}$-in. holes are to be drilled in the ends to receive the pivot pins and the lock pins.

Figure 2-2

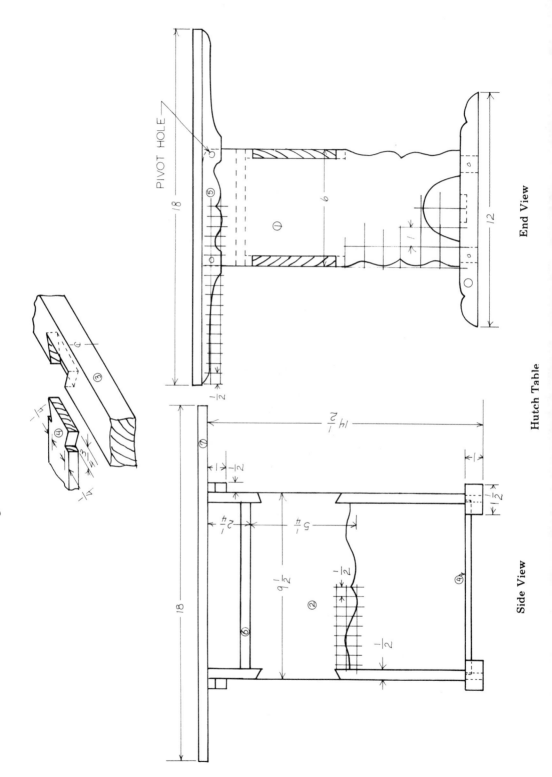

PIVOT HOLE

End View

Hutch Table

Side View

17

22. Shape four pins to secure the top to the base. Let two be pivot pins
    and two be lock pins.

23. The table can now be permanently assembled.

HARVEST TABLE

Some of my fondest memories are about harvest time, when all of the
farmers in the area would go from farm to farm harvesting the wheat.
At the noon hour every one would go to the farmhouse, where a huge
harvest table, laden with food for the workers, would be set up under
the cool shade trees in the yard.

Plate 5 Harvest table. Doll: 31-in.
German.

Bill of Materials

Number required	Part name and number	Size (in.)		
		T X	W X	L
2	Leg (1)	1	2	13
2	Foot (2)	1½	1½	12
2	Brace (3)	1½	1½	15
1	Stretcher (4)	1½	1½	20¾
1	Top (5)	½	15	30

STEPS OF PROCEDURE

1. Select the stock for the legs and cut to the correct size.
2. Cut the tenons on the legs as shown in Figure 2-3. The top and bottom tenons are cut the same.
3. Select the stock for the feet, and cut to size.
4. Select the stock for the braces, and cut to size.
5. Locate the position for the mortises in the feet and braces, and cut to give a tight fit for the tenons on the legs.
6. Select the stock for the stretcher, and cut to size.
7. Cut the tenons on the stretcher as shown in Figure 2-4.
8. Locate the position for the mortise in the legs for the tenons on the stretcher, and cut to give a tight fit for the tenons on the stretchers.
9. Assemble the legs, feet, braces, and stretcher, using glue and pins as shown in the drawings.
10. Select the stock for the top and cut to size.
11. The top can be secured by inserting screws through the braces from the bottom.

CANDLE STAND

The candle stand or tip-top table has a dual purpose. When it is in the upright position, as shown in Plate 6, it can function as a serving table as well as holding a candle. When the top is placed in the vertical position, the small hinge block is large enough to hold a candle, and the top can serve as a shield from any draft that might blow the candle out.

Bill of Materials

Number required	Part name and number	T	X	W	X	L
				Size (in.)		
1	Pedestal (1)	$1\frac{1}{2}$		$1\frac{1}{2}$		$10\frac{5}{8}$
1	Top (2)	$\frac{1}{2}$		$8\frac{3}{4}$		13
3	Leg (3)	$\frac{1}{2}$		3		9
2	Brace (4)	$\frac{1}{2}$		1		8
1	Hinge block (5)	1		3		3

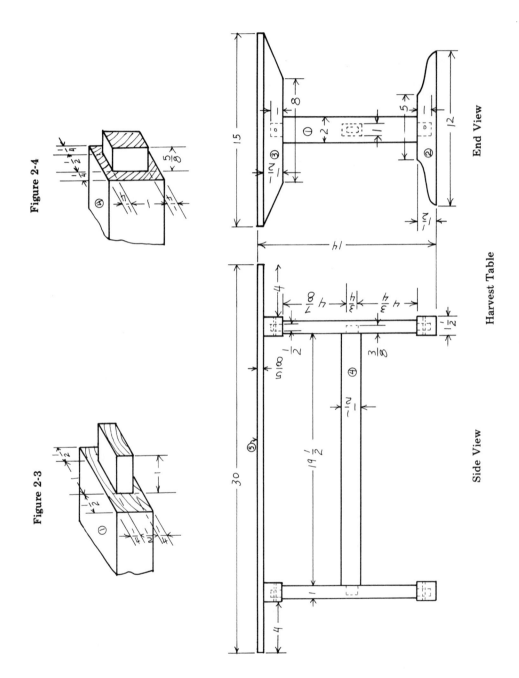

Figure 2-4

Figure 2-3

End View

Harvest Table

Side View

Plate 6 Candle stand. Doll: 31-in.
Simone Halbig.

STEPS OF PROCEDURE

1. Select the stock for the pedestal, cut to the correct size, and turn the lower $1\frac{3}{8}$ in. of the design.
2. Lay out the three full dovetail mortises as shown in Figure 2-5.
3. Cut the mortises up into the pedestal $1\frac{1}{2}$ in.
4. Make a pattern of the legs on $\frac{1}{8}$-in. scrap stock.
5. Select the stock for the legs, and placing the pattern on the stock for the most strength, trace and cut to shape.
6. Assign to each leg one of the mortises that have been cut in the pedestal, and individually cut a dovetail joint in each leg to fit its assigned mortise. Trial-fit the joints as you work them.

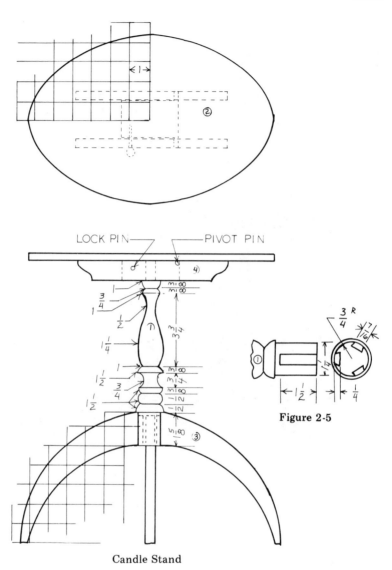

Figure 2-5

Candle Stand

7. Place the pedestal on the lathe and complete the turning of the design.

8. Select the stock for the hinge block, and cut to the overall correct size.

9. Bore a ½-in. hole in the center of the block.

10. Cut the length back ½ in. from both ends, leaving stock to form the two pivot pins as shown in Figure 2-6.

Figure 2-6

11. Trial fit the hinge block on the dowel that has been turned at the top of the pedestal.
12. Select the stock for the top and cut to the correct size and shape.
13. Select the stock for the braces, and cut to the correct size and shape.
14. Position the braces on the bottom surface of the top as illustrated by dashed lines on the top view.
15. Position the pedestal in the center of the top, and mark where the pivot holes are to be bored in the braces to receive the pivot pins on the block. I recommend that you practice on a scrap block to see where the hole needs to be with respect to the edge of the braces.
16. Bore the holes for the pivot pins, and assemble the hinge block and braces.
17. Bore a hole through the brace 2 in. from where the pivot hole is bored, and into the hinge block. This hole will receive a lock pin to prevent the top from tipping when in the horizontal position (top view).
18. Attach the braces to the top by placing screws up through the braces into the top.
19. Permanently glue the legs onto the pedestal.

GATELEG TABLE

The eating table has always been one place in the home where all of the family members gathered for food and conversation, or where someone could enjoy a quiet moment with a cup of tea. This is a very popular type of table because it takes up so little space when not in use.

Plate 7   Gateleg table. Doll: 23-in. German special.

Bill of Materials

Number required	Part name and number	Size (in.)				
		T	X	W	X	L
6	Leg (1)	1½		1½		14½
2	Side rail (2)	½		2		17½
2	End rail (3)	½		2		8
2	Swing rail (4)	½		2		7⅞
2	Anchor rail (5)	½		2		7⅞
1	Top (6)	½		10		20
2	Leaf (7)	½		9		20

STEPS OF PROCEDURE

1. Select the stock for the legs and cut to the correct size.
2. Lay out the mortises to receive the tenons that are to be on the rails. See Figure 2-7. (The side rails must be in from the outer face of the leg ½ in. See the top view.)
3. Select the stock for the side and end rails, and cut to the correct size.
4. Cut a ¼-in.-thick by 1½-in.-long tenon on the ends of the rails and fit to the mortises in the legs.

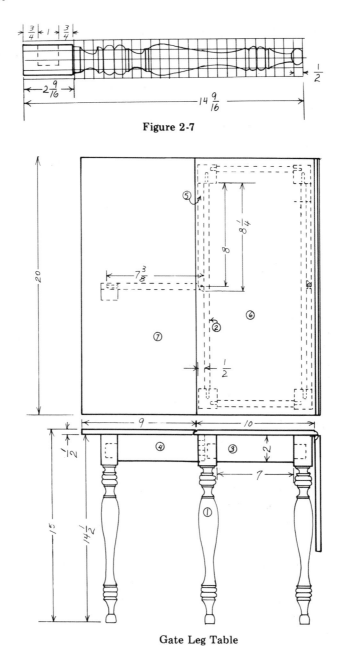

Figure 2-7

Gate Leg Table

5. Turn the design on the legs as shown in Figure 2-7.

6. Trial-assemble the frame of legs.

7. Select the stock for the anchor rail and the swing rail.

8. Cut the knuckle joint as shown in Figure 2-8.

9. Cut a tenon on the end of the swing rail that will carry the gateleg.

10. Cut a mortise in the gateleg to receive the tenon so that the outer face of the swing rail will be flush with the outer surface of the gateleg.

11. Carefully notch the top of the gateleg so that it will go under the side rail when the leg is up under the table top. Be sure to notch the legs so that they swing out from opposite ends of the table. See Figure 2-9.

12. Trial-assemble the anchor rail, swing rail, and gateleg.

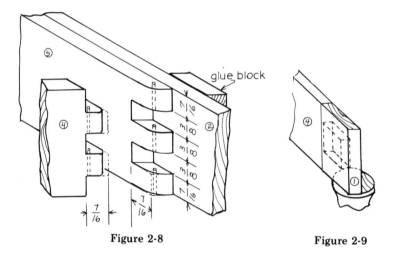

Figure 2-8   Figure 2-9

13. Clamp a gateleg assembly to each side rail, and check to be sure that the gateleg swings freely.

14. Select the stock for the top, and cut to size.

15. Select the stock for the leafs, and cut to size.

16. Fit the top to the leafs by cutting a rule joint as shown in Figure 2-10. You may wish to practice this joint on scrap wood. When placing the hinge, the barrel of the hinge must be set down into the wood flush. When the leaf is lowered or raised, there should not be a crack between the top and the leaf.

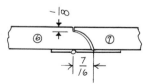

17. The frame of legs, and the gateleg assembly, may now be assembled permanently.
18. Attach the top with glue blocks as shown in Figure 2-8.

Chapter 3

Beds and Mirror

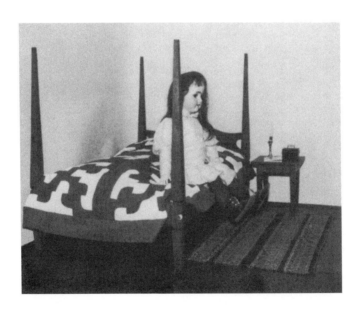

PENCIL POST BED

After a difficult day, the bed becomes a welcome place for a weary person. However, the young girl shown may have been naughty, and must think for a while.

Bill of Materials

Number required	Part name and number	Size (in.)		
		T X	W X	L
4	Post (1)	$1\frac{1}{2}$	$1\frac{1}{2}$	30
2	End rail (2)	$\frac{3}{4}$	$2\frac{1}{2}$	25
2	Side rail (3)	$\frac{3}{4}$	$2\frac{1}{2}$	37
1	Headboard (4)	$\frac{3}{4}$	6	25

STEPS OF PROCEDURE

1. Select the stock for the post, and cut to the correct size.
2. Locate the positions for the mortises, and lay out and cut as shown in Figure 3-1. This includes the mortises for the headboard.
3. Using a band saw, cut the V-shaped design in the post as shown in the front view.
4. Cut the upper and lower tapers on the post as shown in the front view.
5. Select the stock for the headboard and end rails, and cut to the correct size.
6. Lay out and cut a $\frac{3}{8}$-in.-thick by 2-in.-wide and $\frac{3}{4}$-in.-long tenon on each end of the end rails.

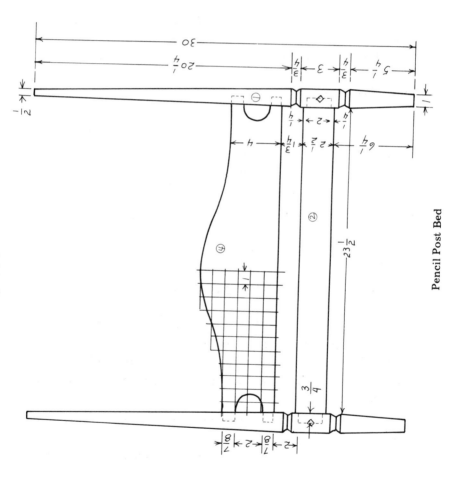

Figure 3-1

Pencil Post Bed

7. Assemble the end rail and two posts that have been chosen to serve as the posts for the head of the bed.

8. With the head post assembled in what will be the permanent position, align the headboard stock in the proper position, and scribe the slope of the taper on the headboard stock. This will identify the location of the shoulders of the tenons that are to be cut on the headboard.

9. Using the measurement between the mortises cut in the post, locate and lay out the design on the ends of the headboard as shown in the front view.

10. Cut the design in the headboard stock.

11. Cut four $\frac{3}{4}$-in.-thick by $\frac{7}{8}$-in.-wide tenons to the length of the tapered shoulder defined in step 6.

12. Trial-assemble the headboard of the bed.

13. Trial-assemble the footboard of the bed.

14. Select the stock for the side rails, and cut to the correct size.

Note: The bed may be assembled permanently by gluing the footboard assembly and the headboard assembly as well as the side rails. I would recommend that you attach the side rails to the post with $\frac{1}{4}$-in. by $1\frac{1}{2}$-in.-lag screws. This will allow for diassembling of the bed for storage.

ROPE BED

When traveling across country in a wagon, space was at a premium and bed springs were only for the well-to-do. To provide a method of supporting the bedding on the bedstead, and also to make it convenient to move, ropes were stretched across the bed from rail to rail, forming a net. Most early bedsteads could be completely disassembled, for ease in transport.

Bill of Materials

Number required	Part name and number	Size (in.)		
		T X	W X	L

4	Post (1)	2	2	$21\frac{1}{2}$
2	End rail (2)	$1\frac{3}{4}$	$1\frac{3}{4}$	20
2	Side rail (3)	$1\frac{3}{4}$	$1\frac{3}{4}$	30
1	Headboard (4)	$\frac{3}{4}$	13	20
1	Blanket roll (5)	$1\frac{1}{2}$	$1\frac{1}{2}$	20

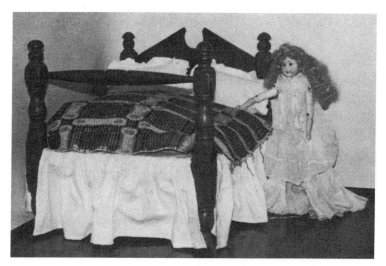

Plate 9   Rope bed. Doll: 21-in. German.

STEPS OF PROCEDURE

1. Select the stock for the post, and cut to the correct size.
2. Locate the mortises in the post for the rails and the headboard. Be sure to lay out the mortises for left and right head posts and left and right foot posts.
3. Cut the mortises in the posts, and bore $\frac{3}{4}$-in. holes in the foot posts to receive the blanket roll.
4. Turn the design on the post as shown in Figure 3-2.
5. Select the stock for the end rails and side rails, and cut to the correct size.
6. Cut the mortises on the ends of the rails as shown in Figure 3-3.
7. Select the stock for the headboard, and cut to the correct size.

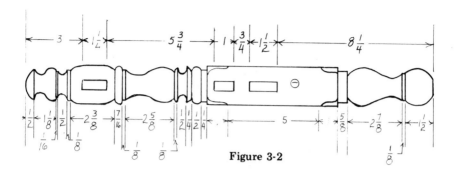

Figure 3-2

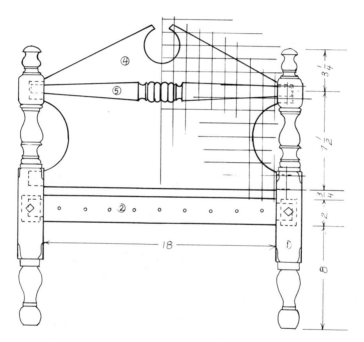

Rope Bed

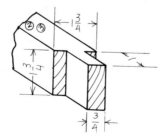

Figure 3-3

8. Lay out the design on the ends of the headboard so that the tenons will fit into the mortises cut in the post for the headboard.

9. At this time cut only the end design on the headboard.

10. Cut the tenons in the headboard to fit the mortises in the post.

11. Cut the remaining design in the headboard.

12. Select the stock for the blanket roll, and turn according to the design shown in the front view.

13. Trial-assemble the bed frame.

14. If the bed is to be a rope bed, drill $\frac{3}{8}$-in. holes evenly spaced in the end and side rails.

15. If the bed is to be a slat bed, glue $\frac{3}{4}$-in.-square strips along the inside bottom edge of the side rails to support the bedding.

TRUNDLE BED

The small cabins common in colonial America had to be used in the most effective way. One way was to have furnishings that could be placed out of the way when not in use. The trundle bed provided a place for the children to sleep, and could be pushed under the big bed during the day.

Plate 10   Trundle bed. Dolls: 9-in. twins.

Bill of Materials

		Size (in.)				
Number required	Part name and number	T	X	W	X	L
4	Post (1)	1½		1½		7¼
2	End rail (2)	1		1		14
2	Roll (3)	1		1		14
2	Side rail (4)	1		1		20

STEPS OF PROCEDURE

1. Select the stock for the post, and lay out the mortises as shown in Figure 3-4.
2. Cut the mortises ¾-in. deep.

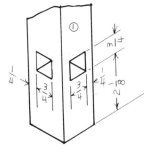

Figure 3-4

3. Locate the position for the ½-in. holes on the post to receive the rolls, and bore.
4. Turn the design on the post stock as shown in the front view.
5. Select the stock for the rails, cut to the correct size, and cut the tenons on the ends of each rail as illustrated in Figure 3-5.
6. Select the stock for the rolls, cut to the correct size, and turn the design as shown in the front view.
7. Locate the positions of the holes for the roping, and drill. The holes should be approximately ¼ in., depending on the size of rope used.

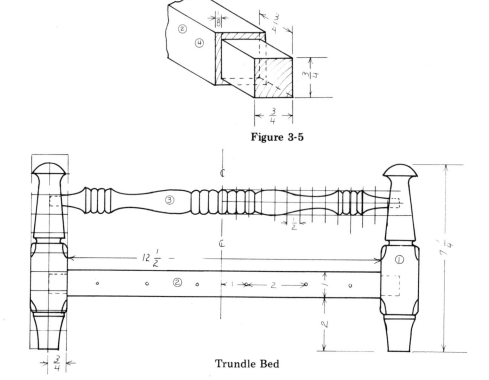

Figure 3-5

Trundle Bed

8. The bedstead can now be assembled. If permanent assembly is desired, use glue. If you want to be able to take the bedstead apart, peg the mortise and tenons or use lag screws.

CRADLE

At last the child sleeps, knowing well that love and kindness watches over. Now mother can have a few moments alone to get other chores done.

Bill of Materials

Number required	Part name and number	Size (in.)		
		T X	W X	L
2	Head post (1)	$\frac{5}{8}$	$\frac{5}{8}$	9
2	Foot post (2)	$\frac{5}{8}$	$\frac{5}{8}$	8
2	Side (3)	$\frac{3}{8}$	$5\frac{1}{2}$	$14\frac{1}{2}$

1	Headboard (4)	$\frac{3}{8}$	7	7
1	Footboard (5)	$\frac{3}{8}$	6	7
2	Rocker (6)	$\frac{1}{4}$	$1\frac{1}{2}$	11

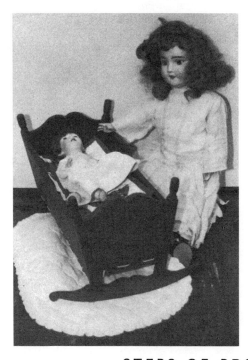

Plate 11　Cradle. Dolls: 22-in. German, 9-in. character baby.

STEPS OF PROCEDURE

1. Select the stock for the head board and foot board, and cut to the size and shape shown in Figures 3-6 and 3-7.
2. Lay out bareface tenons $\frac{1}{4}$-in thick and $3\frac{1}{4}$-in. wide with the shoulder on the outside. (See Chapter 1 for a description of the bareface tenon.)
3. Cut the bareface tenons on the headboard and footboard stock.
4. Select the stock for the head post and foot post.
5. Lay out for the mortises, as shown in Figure 3-8, so that the outside face of the headboard, footboard, and sides will be flush with the outside surface of the posts.
6. Cut the mortises in the four posts as shown in Figure 3-8. Do not cut the slots for the rockers.
7. Place the post on the lathe and turn the knobs as shown in Figure 3-9.

Figure 3-6 & Figure 3-7

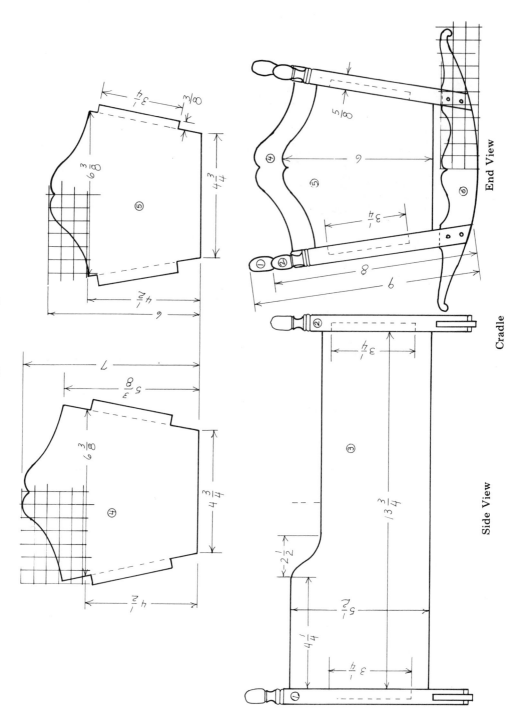

Cradle

End View

Side View

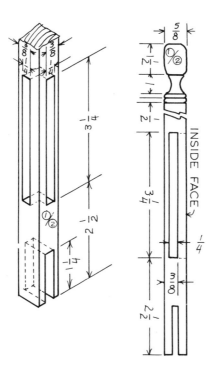

Figure 3-8 & Figure 3-9

8. Select the stock for the sides, cut to the correct size, and lay out and cut a ¼-in. by 3¼-in. bareface tenon on each end of the side stock. Place the shoulder of the tenons on the outside surface.

9. Trial-assemble the parts.

10. Select the stock for the rockers, and cut as shown in the end view.

11. Align the rockers with the post, and mark the rocker height on the post.

12. Disassemble the cradle and cut a ¼-in.-wide slit up into the ends of the post as far as the rocker will go according to the marks made in step 11.

13. Drill holes along the bottom edge of the sides, headboard, and footboard if you intend to make the cradle a rope type; otherwise, glue ½-in.-square pieces along the inside bottom edge to hold slats for the bedding.

14. Assemble the cradle using glue in the mortise-and-tenon joints.

15. Secure the rockers using wood pins to hold them in place.

DRESSING MIRROR

She is not vain; she only wishes to look nice. With such a beautiful face, who can blame her for wanting to look in a mirror? The dressing mirror was a very important part of the Victorian woman's dressing room.

Plate 12   Dressing mirror. Doll: 22-22-in. china head.

Bill of Materials

Number required	Part name and number	Size (in.)		
		T	X W X	L
2	Post (1)	$\frac{1}{2}$	$1\frac{1}{2}$	$19\frac{1}{2}$
2	Foot (2)	$\frac{1}{2}$	2	8
1	Stretcher (3)	$\frac{3}{4}$	$1\frac{1}{2}$	11
1	Frame stock (4)	$\frac{1}{2}$	$\frac{3}{4}$	42
1	Crown (5)	$\frac{1}{2}$	$2\frac{1}{2}$	$9\frac{1}{2}$
2	Finial (6)	$\frac{1}{2}$	$\frac{1}{2}$	$3\frac{1}{4}$

STEPS OF PROCEDURE

1. Select the stock for the post, and cut the tenons on the bottom as shown.
2. Select the stock for the stretcher, cut to the correct size, and cut the tenons on both ends. Notice that the tenons pass through the entire thickness of the post.
3. Cut a mortise in the post through the entire thickness of the post to receive the tenons on the stretcher.
4. Select the stock for the feet, but do not cut the design at this time.
5. Cut the mortises in the feet to receive the tenons on the post.
6. Trial-assemble the post, feet, and stretcher.
7. Disassemble the pieces.
8. Cut the taper on the post, and drill a ¼-in. hole down into the top of the post to receive the finale.
9. Cut the design on the feet.
10. Select the stock for the finials, and turn as shown in Figure 3-10.

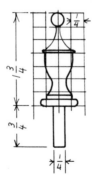

Figure 3-10

11. Select stock for the frame, and form the design as shown in Figure 3-11.
12. Select the stock for the crown, and cut the pattern as shown in the front view.
13. Cut the frame stock and crown to the correct dimensions, and assemble using miter joints on the corners. (These joints should be reinforced with splines or small brads.)
14. Drill 5/32-in. holes in the post as shown on the front view.
15. Holding the mirror frame in place, drill ⅛-in. holes in frame sides.
16. The post, feet, and stretcher may be assembled permanently.

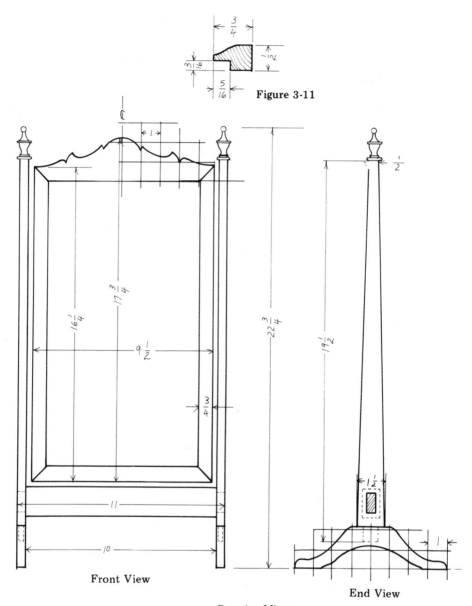

Figure 3-11

Front View

End View

Dressing Mirror

17. Place the mirror glass in the frame.
18. Place a metal pin through the hole in the post into the hole in the frame. The pin should fit snug in the post but rather tight in the frame. (A round-head brass wood screw may be used instead of a pin.)
19. Glue the finials in place.

Chapter 4

Chests

BLANKET CHEST

The blanket chest shown is an example of the first step toward what became known as a chest of drawers. For many years our forefathers placed their belongings in boxes or chests. Some of these chests had a smaller box inside called a tile. We are not sure when it happened, but eventually someone, weary of having to dig to the bottom of a chest for a piece of clothing or other article, decided to put a false bottom in the chest and have a pull-out section under the false bottom. With this the concept of the drawer was developed. When this was done the chest was made taller. To break up the massive appearance of a plain front, molding such as that shown on the chest in this article was nailed on the front to give the illusion of many drawers or partitions. Eventually, more drawers were added, giving us the chest of drawers.

Bill of Materials

Number required	Part name and number	Size (in.)		
		T ×	W ×	L
2	End (1)	½	8	16
1	Bottom (2)	½	7½	18½
1	Partition (3)	½	7	18½
1	Front (4)	½	7	19
1	Back (5)	½	12	18½
1	Top (6)	½	8⅝	20
1	Drawer front	½	4½	18
2	Drawer side	½	4½	7¼
1	Drawer back	½	4	18
1	Drawer bottom	¼	7½	18½

Partition molding	¼	½	65
Base molding	½	½	36

STEPS OF PROCEDURE

1. Select the stock for the ends, and cut to the correct size.
2. Lay out the joints as illustrated in Figure 4-1, being sure to lay out for a left end and a right end.
3. Cut the two dado joints first.
4. Cut the ¼-in. by ½-in. rabbet joint on the back inside edge as shown.
5. Cut the notch on the front edge that is to receive the front board.
6. Cut the foot design as shown in the end view.
7. Select the stock for the partition and the bottom, and cut to the correct size.
8. Select the stock for the back and cut to the correct size.
9. Permanently assemble the ends, the partition, the bottom, and the back piece.
10. Select the stock for the front and cut to the correct size.
11. Attach the front to the chest, using glue and nails.
12. Select the stock for the base mold, and form as shown in the cross-sectional view in Figure 4-2.
13. Attach the base mold to the chest with small nails. Use miter joints at the corners.
14. Select the stock for the partition mold, and form as shown in the cross-sectional view in Figure 4-3.
15. Temporarily place the molding on the outer edges of the chest.
16. Place the piece of partition molding above the drawer, joining the pieces of molding as shown in Figure 4-4.
17. Place the remaining pieces of partition molding as shown in the front view.
18. When all of the partition moldings are properly fitted, the pieces may be permanently fastened with glue and very small wire brads.
19. Select the stock for the top, and cut to the correct size.
20. Secure the top using butt hinges.
21. Construct the drawer using either the dado method or the dovetail method. Both methods were discussed in Chapter 1.

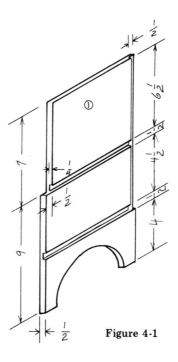

Figure 4-1

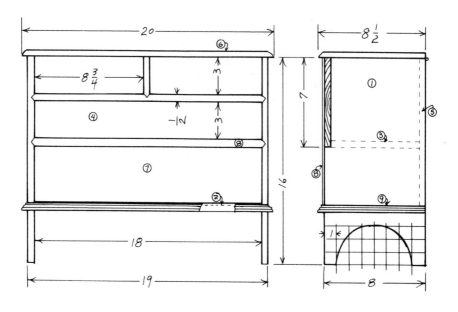

Front View

End View

Blanket Chest

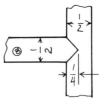

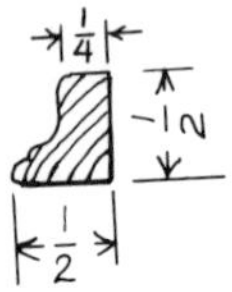

Figure 4-2 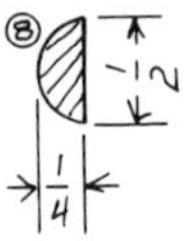   Figure 4-3   Figure 4-4

SIX-BOARD BLANKET CHEST

The blanket chest was and still is an ideal place for a person to keep special things. As the young woman arranges her belongings, she seems to be pausing for a moment either to remember the past or contemplate the future.

Plate 14 Six-board blanket chest. Doll: 23-in. C. M. Berginarn.

Bill of Materials

Number required	Part name and number	Size (in.)		
		T ×	W ×	L
2	Side (1)	½	5¼	13¼
2	End (2)	½	5¼	8½
1	Bottom (3)	⅝	8¾	13¾
1	Top (4)	⅝	8¾	13¾
4	Foot (5)	1¼	1¼	2⅜

STEPS OF PROCEDURE

1. Select the stock for the ends and sides, and cut to the correct size.
2. Lay out the dovetails as shown in Figure 4-5.
3. Cut the dovetails in the end stock.
4. Identify the ends and sides so that you will always be fitting the pieces in the same array.
5. Using the dovetails that were cut in the end stock as individual patterns, cut mortises in the side stock to match a specific dovetail array. *Note:* If you do not wish to cut the dovetails, you may use the rabbet joint, as shown in Chapter 1.
6. Assemble the box portion of the chest.
7. Select the stock for the top and bottom, and cut to the correct size.
8. Round the front and two ends of the bottom, and bore $\frac{1}{2}$-in. holes in the bottom to receive the feet. See the front and end views.
9. Select the stock for the feet and turn as shown in Figure 4-6.
10. Attach the bottom to the box of the chest, using small-headed nails and glue.
11. Attach the top to the box using small butt hinges.
12. Glue the feet in place.

SEVENTEENTH-CENTURY CHEST OF DRAWERS

The construction of the chest of drawers shown follows the example of the early seventeenth-century type of construction. The method is rather simple in that the dado joints that are cut in the end stock are through dado joints; that is, the joints are exposed on the front edge of the end stock. To hide these joints, a half-round molding is placed on the outside edge of the chest, and a base molding is placed around the bottom of the chest to provide a logical termination for the vertical mold. Also, the drawer dividers have molding that joins with the vertical pieces with a 45-degree butt joint. As is typical for a chest of this period, the rear foot is an extension of the end stock, while the front foot is an elaborately turned foot.

The drawer pulls should be a drop pull. Being unable to find a miniature of this type of pull, I fabricated pulls from small pieces of brass and wire.

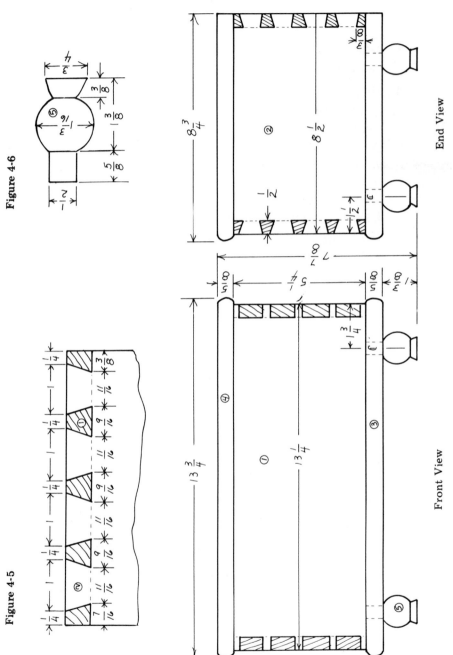

Figure 4-6

Figure 4-5

Six Board Blanket Chest

End View

Front View

Plate 15 17th century chest of drawers. Doll: 22-in. German.

Bill of Materials

Number required	Part name and number	Size (in.)		
		T X	W X	L
2	End (1)	½	8	15
4	Divider (2)	½	7¼	16
1	Bottom (3)	½	7¼	16
1	Top (4)	½	8⅝	17¼
1	Drawer front (5)	½	2¼	15½
1	Drawer front (6)	½	2¼	15½
1	Drawer front (7)	½	3	15½
1	Drawer front (8)	½	3	15½
4	Drawer side	½	2¼	7½
4	Drawer side	½	3	7½
2	Drawer back	½	1⅜	18⅛
2	Drawer back	½	2½	15⅛
4	Drawer bottom	¼	13½	15

2	Leg (9)	$1\frac{1}{4}$	$1\frac{1}{4}$	$2\frac{1}{2}$
1	Back (10)	$\frac{1}{4}$	$13\frac{1}{2}$	16
1	Base mold stock (11)	$\frac{1}{2}$	$\frac{3}{8}$	28
1	Trim stock (12)	$\frac{1}{4}$	$\frac{1}{2}$	90

STEPS OF PROCEDURE

1. Select the stock for the ends, and cut to the correct size.
2. Locate the position for the dado joints that are to receive the bottom and the four dividers. Be sure to mark off a right and left end. See Figure 4-7.

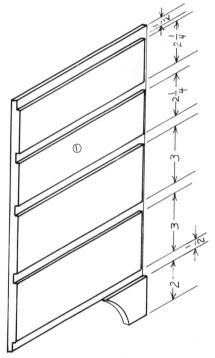

Figure 4-7

3. Cut the dado joints $\frac{1}{2}$-in. wide and $\frac{1}{4}$-in. deep.
4. Cut a $\frac{1}{4}$-in. by $\frac{1}{4}$-in. rabbet joint on the inside rear corners of the ends to receive the back stock.
5. Cut the design for the rear foot as shown in the end view.
6. Select the stock for the bottom and the four dividers, cut to the correct size.
7. Trial-assemble the ends, the dividers, and the bottom.

8. Select the stock for the front feet, and turn as shown in Figure 4-8.

9. Remove the bottom from the trial assembly, and bore ½-in. holes in the bottom as shown in Figure 4-10, to receive the dowel that has been turned on the front feet.

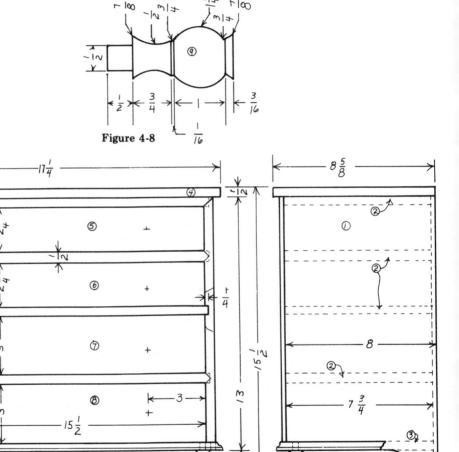

Figure 4-8

Seventeenth-Century Chest of Drawers

Front View   End View

Figure 4-10

10. Permanently assemble the parts obtained thus far, using glue and small-headed nails.

11. Glue the front feet in place.

12. Select the stock for the top and cut to the correct size.

13. The top can be placed on the chest permanently by gluing to the top divider.

14. Select the fronts for all of the drawers, and individually fit the fronts to the perspective opening. Be sure to identify where each front fits.

15. Select the stock for drawer sides, backs, and bottoms. These parts are not shown.

16. Following the dado type of drawer construction discussed in Chapter 1, construct the drawers for the chest.

17. Select the stock for the base molding, and shape as shown in Figure 4-9a.

Figure 4-9 (a and b)

18. Secure the base mold to the chest with small-headed nails. Use miter joints at the corners.

19. Select the stock for the back and secure to the chest with small-headed nails.

20. Secure the stock for the half-round edge mold as shown in Figure 4-9b, and trim out the front of the chest as shown in the front view.

21. Select the type of pulls for the drawers and attach.

AMERICAN EMPIRE CHEST OF DRAWERS

The American Empire chest has the very distinctive feature that the top drawer protrudes beyond the lower drawers, forming a ledge whereby a split column can be placed down the sides of the front of the chest. The chest shown is a simpler version of the American Empire style in that the split columns are not included.

Plate 16   American empire chest of drawers. Doll: 31-in. German.

Bill of Materials

Number required	Part name and number	Size (in.)		
		T ×	W ×	L
4	Post (1)	1	1	20½
2	End top rail (2)	½	2½	8½
2	End bottom rail (3)	½	2	8½
3	Drawer divider (4)	½	1	19
2	Drawer divider (5)	½	1½	19
8	Drawer support (6)	½	2	8⅜
2	End panel (7)	¼	8⅜	13½
1	Rear bottom stretcher (8)	½	2	19
1	Rear top stretcher (9)	½	2½	19
1	Back panel (10)	¼	13½	18½
1	Drawer front (11)	½	4½	18
1	Drawer front (12)	½	3	18
1	Drawer front (13)	½	3½	18
1	Drawer front (14)	½	4	18
2	Drawer side (15)	½	4½	9¼
1	Drawer back (16)	½	3⅝	18
2	Drawer side (17)	½	3	8⅞

1	Drawer back (18)	½	2½	18
2	Drawer side (19)	½	3½	8⅞
1	Drawer back (20)	½	2⅝	18
2	Drawer side (21)	½	4	8⅞
1	Drawer back (22)	½	3	18
1	Drawer bottom (23)	¼	9	17½
3	Drawer bottom (24)	¼	8½	7½
1	Top (25)	½	10¼	21
8	Drawer guide (26)	½	½	7½
2	Extension block (27)	½	1	6

STEPS OF PROCEDURE

1. Select the stock for the four posts and cut to the correct size, and turn the foot as shown in Figure 4-11.

Figure 4-11

2. Identify two of the posts as the front posts, and lay out the ½-in. by ½-in. by ⅝-in.-deep mortises, as shown in Figure 4-12, to receive the drawer dividers. Be sure to do a left post and a right post.

3. Identify the remaining posts as the rear left and rear right posts, and lay out the mortises for the end rails and the rear stretchers on all of the posts, as shown in Figure 4-13.

4. Cut the mortises for the rails and stretchers.

5. Cut the ¼-in. groove in the post to receive the end panels and back panels, as shown in Figure 4-13.

6. Shape and glue the two blocks on the front face of the front posts as shown in Figure 4-12.

7. Select the stock for the end rails and cut to size.

8. Cut the tenons on the end rails to fit the mortises that have been cut in the posts.

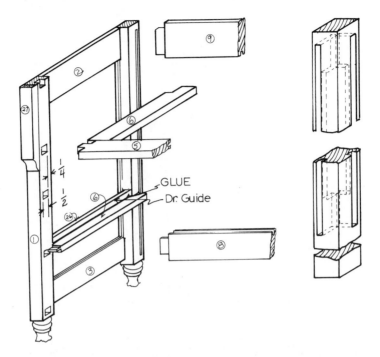

Figure 4-12   Figure 4-13

9. Select the stock for the drawer dividers and the rear stretchers, and cut to the correct size.

10. Cut the tenons on the dividers and stretchers to fit the mortises that have been cut in the posts.

11. On the inside edge of the drawer dividers, cut a groove ¼ in. wide and ¼ in. deep. See Figure 4-14.

12. Trial-assemble the carcass of the chest of drawers.

13. Select the stock for the drawer supports, and cut to the correct size.

14. On the front end of each support, cut a tenon ¼ in. thick and ¼ in. long, as shown in Figure 4-14.

15. Slip the tenon on the support into the groove that has been cut in the back edge of the divider, position against the end of the chest, and mark against the rear leg the exact position for the notch on the end of the support. Mark the position of each support.

16. The tenon on the front of the drawer support will also require notching to fit against the front post.

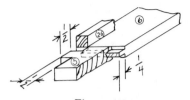

Figure 4-14

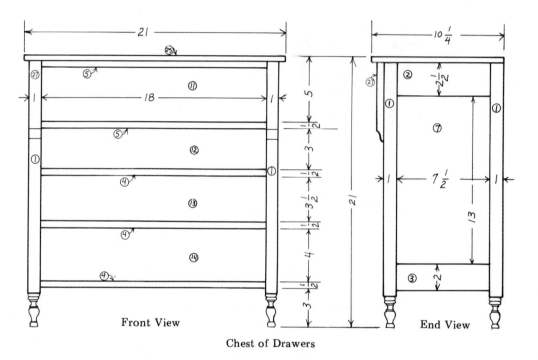

Front View

End View

Chest of Drawers

17. Mark on each end rail and each back stretcher the inside edge that is to have a groove cut to receive a panel.

18. Disassemble the carcass, and cut a groove ¼-in. wide and ⅜-in. deep in the edges of the rails and stretchers that have been marked.

19. Select the stock for the end and back panels, and cut to fit.

20. Permanently assemble the ends of the chest.

21. Permanently join the ends by gluing the stretchers and drawer dividers in place. Be sure that the carcass is square and that the back panel is in place.

22. Glue the drawer supports in place, being sure that they are at 90 degrees off the face of the drawer dividers.

23. Glue ½-in. by ½-in. drawer guides flush with the inside face of the post and placed between the post. See Figure 4-12.

24. Select the stock for the drawer fronts, and cut to fit the proper openings.

25. Select the stock for the drawer sides and backs, and assemble the drawers using either dovetails or the dado method shown in Chapter 1.

26. Select the stock for the top and cut to the correct size.

27. Secure the top to the carcass by gluing it to the top edges of the top rails, rear top stretcher, and the top drawer divider.

Chapter 5

Cabinets and Cupboards

PEWTER CABINET

P̲ewter was the poor man's silver. The rather simply constructed cabinet holding this woman's prized possessions lends itself well to the surroundings.

Bill of Materials

Number required	Part name and number	Size (in.)		
		T ×	W ×	L
2	End (1)	½	8	40
2	Front board (2)	½	4	16
1	Door (3)	½	12	15½
1	Shelf (4)	½	2¾	19½
1	Shelf (5)	½	2½	19½
1	Shelf (6)	½	2½	19½
1	Work top (7)	½	7¾	19½
1	Shelf (8)	½	7¾	19½
1	Bottom (9)	½	7¾	19½
1	Face board (10)	½	1¾	19
1	Top (11)	½	7¾	19½
1	Crown stock (12)	¾	1	40
1	Base mold (13)	½	½	40
	Back stock	¼	random	40

STEPS OF PROCEDURE

1. Select the stock for the end, and cut to the correct size.
2. Locate the position for the dado joints to receive the shelves, bottom, and top.

3. Cut the dado joints, being sure to cut a left end and a right end.

4. Cut a ¼-in. by ¼-in. rabbet joint on the inside rear corner of each end to receive the back. See Figure 5-1.

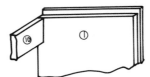

Figure 5-1

5. Cut the cove design in the ends as shown in the end view.

6. Select the stock for the bottom, the top, the work top, and shelf number 8.

7. Temporarily assemble the ends, top, bottom, the work top, and the shelf.

8. Select the stock for the remaining shelves, individually fit them in their proper positions, and number them.

9. Disassemble the work, and in each shelf and work top cut a plate groove 1 in. from the back edge the full length of each piece.

10. Permanently assemble the carcass of the cabinet.

11. Select the stock for the front boards, cut to size, and secure to the front of the cabinet with small-headed nails.

12. Select the stock for the face board, cut to the correct width and the proper length to provide a snug fit between the ends at the very top of the cabinet. Secure the face board by driving nails through the end stock into the end grain of the face boards.

13. Select the stock for the bottom mold and shape as shown in Figure 5-2.

14. Secure the mold to the cabinet, using miter joints at the corners.

15. Select the stock for the door and cut to fit the opening between the front boards. The top of the door should be flush with the top of the work top.

16. Using flush butt hinges, secure the door to the cabinet.

17. Carve a turnbuckle to hold the door closed. Refer to Chapter 1.

18. Select stock for the crown mold and shape as shown in Figure 5-3.

19. Secure the crown mold to the cabinet, using miter joints at the corners.

20. Select the stock for the back, and cut to length equal to the full height of the cabinet.

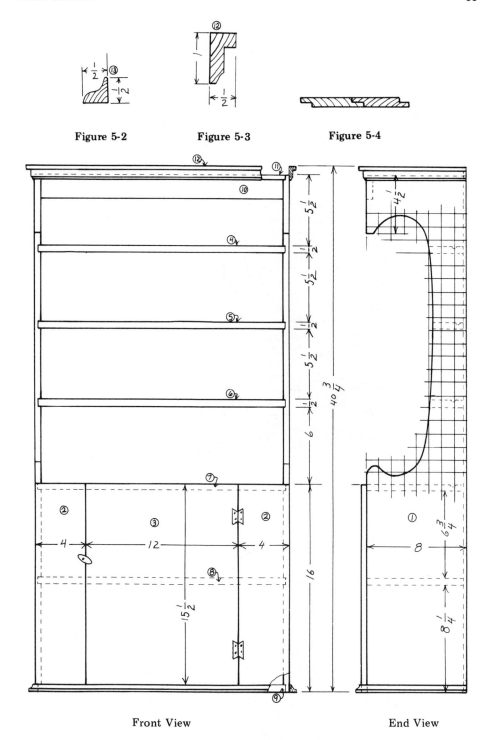

Figure 5-2   Figure 5-3   Figure 5-4

Front View   End View

Pewter Cabinet

21. Cut lap joints in the edges as shown in Figure 5-4.

22. Secure the back stock with small-headed nails.

STEP-BACK CUPBOARD

The step-back cupboard was, and still is, a very popular piece of furniture. Not only does it provide a place to store dishes, it also provides a work surface.

Plate 18 Step-back cupboard. Doll: 31-in. Simone Halbig.

Bill of Materials

Number required	Part name and number	Size (in.)		
		T ×	W ×	L
2	End (1)	½	8½	39¾
4	Shelf (2)	½	4¾	20
1	Top (2)	½	4¾	20
1	Shelf (3)	½	8¼	20
1	Bottom (4)	½	8¼	20
2	Upper stile (5)	½	1½	20³⁄₁₆
1	Upper stretcher (6)	½	2	19½
2	Lower stile (7)	½	2	19⅛
1	Lower stretcher (8)	½	1¼	19½
1	Step top (9)	⁷⁄₁₆	4½	21

4	Upper door stile (10)	$\frac{1}{2}$	$1\frac{1}{2}$	$18\frac{3}{16}$
2	Door rail (11)	$\frac{1}{2}$	$1\frac{1}{2}$	$7\frac{3}{4}$
2	Door divider (12)	$\frac{1}{2}$	$1\frac{1}{2}$	$7\frac{3}{4}$
2	Door rail (13)	$\frac{1}{2}$	2	$7\frac{3}{4}$
4	Lower door stile (14)	$\frac{1}{2}$	$1\frac{1}{2}$	14
2	Door rail (15)	$\frac{1}{2}$	$1\frac{1}{2}$	$7\frac{3}{4}$
2	Door rail (16)	$\frac{1}{2}$	2	$7\frac{3}{4}$
2	Door panel (17)	$\frac{1}{4}$	$6\frac{3}{4}$	$5\frac{1}{2}$
2	Door panel (18)	$\frac{1}{4}$	$6\frac{3}{4}$	$9\frac{3}{4}$
2	Door panel (19)	$\frac{1}{4}$	$6\frac{3}{4}$	$11\frac{1}{2}$
1	Crown mold stock	1	2	36
1	Back stock	$\frac{1}{4}$	20	$34\frac{3}{4}$

STEPS OF PROCEDURE

1. Select the stock for the ends, and cut to the correct size.
2. Locate the positions for the dado joints, and mark for a right and a left end.
3. Cut the dado joints $\frac{1}{2}$-in. wide and $\frac{1}{4}$-in. deep.
4. Cut the step back into the ends.
5. Cut the foot design as shown in the end view.
6. Cut a $\frac{1}{4}$-in. by $\frac{1}{4}$-in. rabbet joint on the inside rear corner of the ends to receive the back.
7. Select the stock for all of the shelves, top, and bottom, and cut to the correct size.
8. Assemble the carcass of the cupboard, using small-headed nails and glue. (Be sure that the cupboard is square.)
9. Select the stock for the upper stiles and stretcher.
10. Lay out and cut the mortise-and-tenon joint as illustrated in the front view.
11. Select the stock for the step top, and cut to the correct size.
12. Fasten the step top to the carcass. You may use glue blocks as shown, or you may drive small-headed nails through the step top down into the end grain of the end stock.
13. Assemble the upper stile and stretcher assembly, and attach to the carcass of the cupboard.
14. Select the stock for the bottom stiles, and lower stretcher, and cut to the correct size.

15. Lay out and cut the mortise-and-tenon joint as illustrated in the front view.

16. Cut the taper on the bottom end of the stiles to form the feet.

17. Assemble the lower stile and stretcher assembly, and attach to the carcass of the cupboard.

18. Select the stock for the back and fasten to the carcass of the cupboard. Be sure that the cupboard is square.

19. Select the stock for the stiles, dividers, and rails for the doors, and cut to the correct size. The doors should be about $\frac{1}{32}$ in. under size to the openings.

20. Lay out and cut the mortises in the stiles as shown in the front view.

21. Cut the tenons on the rails and dividers as shown to fit the tenons.

22. On the inside edge of the rails, stiles, and dividers, cut a $\frac{1}{4}$-in.- by $\frac{1}{2}$-in.-deep groove to receive the door panels. (See Figure 5-6.)

23. Trial-assemble the door frames and test-fit them to the carcass of the cabinet; then disassemble the door frames.

24. Select the stock for the door panels, cut to the correct size, and reassemble the door frames with the panels in place.

25. Test fit the doors to the carcass again to be sure that the doors are not warped.

26. Permanently assemble the doors.

27. The doors can be secured to the cupboard with small brass butt hinges.

28. Select the stock for the mold, and shape as shown in Figure 5-5.

Figure 5-5

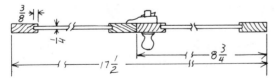

Figure 5-6

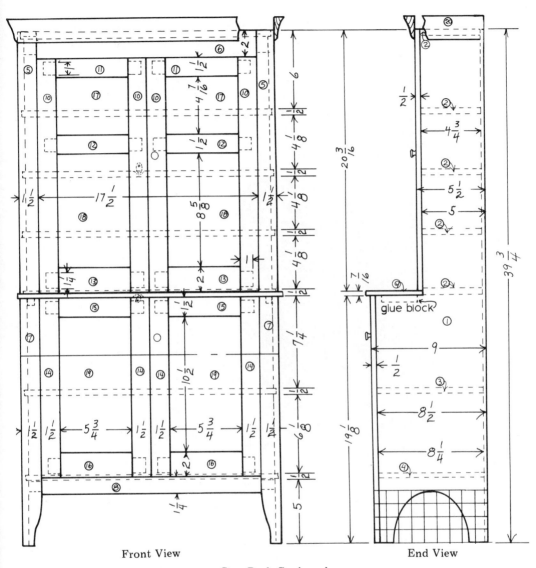

Front View   Step Back Cupboard   End View

CORNER CUPBOARD

The corner cupboard is made of walnut, with whittled door keepers
and knobs. The young woman is busy placing her prized china in a
nice safe place where it can be seen, but is out of the way. The corner

stiles are joined by two 22.5-degree angles being cut on the adjoining edges and held in place with glue and small-headed nails. When constructing a corner cabinet, it is wise to cut the pattern for the shelves and top first. The frame, consisting of the stile assembly, apron, and stretchers, should be made to fit the shelves. In doing so, compensations can be made for any error in dimensions.

Plate 19 Corner cabinet. Doll: 25-in. china head.

Bill of Materials

Number required	Part name and number	Size (in.)		
		T ×	W ×	L
2	Front stile (1)	½	2	37
2	Side stile (2)	½	2	37
4	Shelf (3)	½	9¾	22¼
1	Top (3a)	½	9¾	22¼
1	Bottom (3b)	½	9¾	22¼
1	Top stretcher (4)	½	1¾	18
1	Center stretcher (5)	½	2½	18
1	Apron (6)	½	1⅞	18
Upper doors				
4	Door stile (7)	½	1½	17¾

2	Top rail (8)	$\frac{1}{2}$	$1\frac{1}{2}$	7
2	Bottom rail (9)	$\frac{1}{2}$	$1\frac{3}{4}$	7
2	Door panel (14)	$\frac{1}{4}$	$5\frac{3}{4}$	$15\frac{1}{4}$
Lower doors				
4	Door stile (10)	$\frac{1}{2}$	$1\frac{1}{2}$	13
2	Top rail (11)	$\frac{1}{2}$	$1\frac{1}{2}$	7
2	Bottom rail (12)	$\frac{1}{2}$	$1\frac{3}{4}$	7
2	Door panel (13)	$\frac{1}{4}$	$5\frac{3}{4}$	$10\frac{1}{2}$
1	Rear stile (15)	$\frac{1}{2}$	$4\frac{1}{4}$	37
1	Back stock (16)	$\frac{1}{4}$	random	$35\frac{3}{8}$
1	Molding stock (17)	$\frac{3}{4}$	1	30

STEPS OF PROCEDURE

1. Select the stock for the shelves, top, and bottom, and cut all pieces to the exact shape and size. See Figure 5-9 for the layout pattern.
2. Select the stock for the front stile, side stile, and back stile, and cut to the correct length and width.
3. From the dimensions shown on the front view, locate the position for the dado joints for the shelves, top, and bottom on the side stiles and the back stile. Be sure to lay out a left and a right side when doing the side stiles.
4. Cut the joints $\frac{1}{2}$-in. wide and $\frac{1}{4}$-in. deep. Do this on the back stile and side stiles only.
5. Cut a $\frac{1}{4}$-in. by $\frac{1}{4}$-in. rabbet on the rear inside corner of the side stiles to receive the back stock.
6. Locate the mortises on the front stiles as shown in Figure 5-10. Be sure to lay out for a left side and a right side.
7. Cut the mortises $\frac{1}{4}$-in. wide and 1-in. deep on the center of the inside edge of the front stiles.
8. Cut a 22.5-degree angle on the edges of the front and side stiles that will meet. (This can be accomplished by setting the table saw blade at 67.5 degrees off perpendicular.)
9. Cut five clamping blocks to fit the jointed stiles as shown in Figure 5-8, and glue the left front stile to the left side stile to form the left stile assembly. Repeat this with the right stiles to form the right stile assembly.
10. Temporarily assemble the two front stile assemblies, the rear stile, the top, and the bottom.

11. Very carefully measure the distance between the inside edges of the front stiles. This measurement will be the exact length that the apron and stretchers must measure between the shoulders of the tenons that are to be cut on the apron and stretchers.

12. Select the stock for the stretchers and the apron, cut to the correct width, and cut to a length that is 2 in. greater than the measurement taken in step 11.

13. Lay out a ¼-in.-thick by 1-in.-long tenon on the stretcher and apron, and cut to fit the mortises that have been cut in the stiles.

14. Cut the design on the apron as shown in the front view.

15. The front pieces for the cupboard—the stile assemblies, apron, and stretchers—are ready for final assembly.

16. Fasten the rear stile to the rear edge of the top, bottom, and shelves using small nails.

17. Place the front of the cupboard on the front of the top, bottom, and shelves by fitting the pieces into the dado joints. Secure with glue and small-headed nails.

18. Select the stock for the back and secure to the cupboard.

19. Select the stiles and rails for the upper and lower doors. Be sure to mark each piece as to which door it belongs to.

20. Cut all pieces to the correct size, and lay out the ¼-in. by 1-in. tenons on all the rails. See the front view.

21. Cut the tenons.

22. Lay out all the mortises on the door stiles, and cut to fit the tenons on the rails.

23. Trial-assemble the door frames, and trial-fit to the openings of the cupboard. Also mark the inside edges of the stiles and rails. This will indicate the correct edge where the groove will be cut to receive the door panels.

24. Disassemble the door frames, and cut a ¼-in.-wide by ½-in.-deep groove on the inside edges of the door stiles and rails.

25. Select the stock for the door panels and cut to the correct size.

26. Trial-assemble the complete door assembly, and check for twist or warping.

27. Permanently assemble the doors using glue and wood pegs.

28. The doors may be placed on the cupboard with butt hinges.

29. Select the stock for the crown mold, and shape as shown in Figure 5-7.

30. The mold can be attached to the cabinet with small-headed nails and glue. Use a 22.5-degree joint at the corners.

31. The latcher and knobs may be metal or wooden turnbuckles, as discussed in Chapter 1.

Figure 5-7

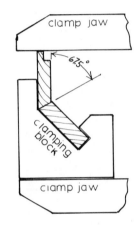

Figure 5-8

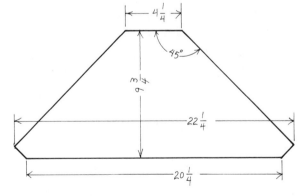

Figure 5-9

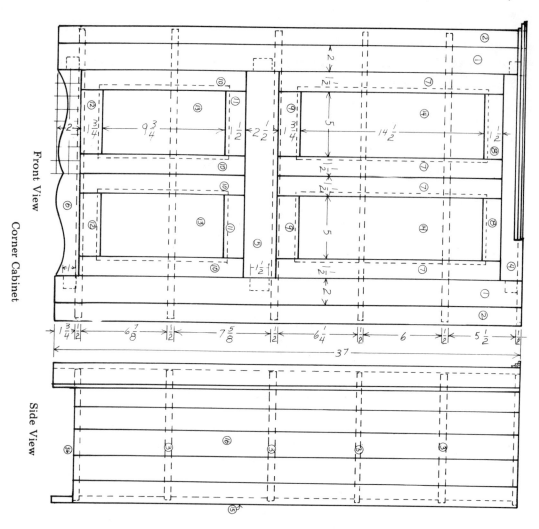

Figure 5-8 (cont.)

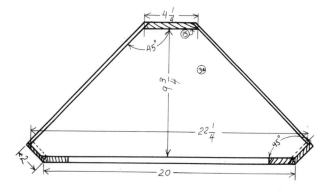

Figure 5-9

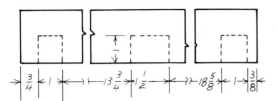

Figure 5-10

Chapter 6

Settle and Chairs

The settle is a large, high-back seat that is used in front of a fireplace. The high back traps the warmth of the fire, and shields the user from cold drafts. The young girl is using the settle as a place to line up her friend and bears for a story.

Bill of Materials

Number required	Part name and number	Size (in.)		
		T X	W X	L
2	End (1)	¾	10	33
1	Apron (2)	¾	5	30
1	Seat (3)	¾	9½	29¼
	Stock for the back (4)	⅜	random	29¼

STEPS OF PROCEDURE

1. Select the stock for the ends, and cut to size.
2. Locate the position for the dado joint that is to hold the seat in place.
3. Cut the ¼-in. by ¾-in. dado on the end stock. Be sure to cut a left end and a right end.
4. Select the stock for the apron, and cut to the correct size.
5. Cut the dovetail joints in the ends of the apron as shown in the front view.
6. Select the stock for the seat, and cut to the correct size.

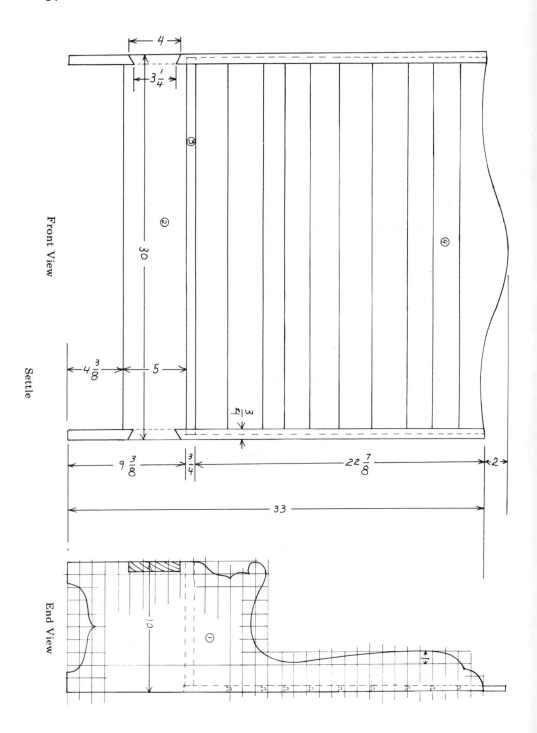

Front View

Settle

End View

7. Trial-assemble the seat and the ends.

8. Position the apron under the seat and using the previously cut dovetails as patterns, scrib a mortise joint on the front edge of the end.

9. Cut the mortises ¾-in. deep to receive the dovetail joints on the apron.

10. Disassemble the ends from the seat, and lay out the design for the feet and arm as shown in the end view.

11. Cut a dado joint ⅜-in. deep and ⅜-in. wide in the back inside corner of the ends to receive the back stock.

12. Cut the design for the feet and the arm on each end piece.

13. Using glue and nails, permanently assemble the seat, ends, and the apron, being sure that the assembly is square.

14. Cut the stock for the back to the correct length.

15. Cut tongue-and-groove joints in the back stock.

16. Secure the back stock to the settle by using at least two screws at each end of each board.

17. Place the top board in place, mark where the ends stop, and lay the design for the top from these points.

18. Cut the design in the top board.

19. Attach the top board to the settle.

Plate 21 Windsor side chairs. Dolls: 29-in. German character, 22-in. German special.

WINDSOR SIDE CHAIR

The Windsor chair was one of our forefathers' most popular forms of seating. Its place in our earlier days is obvious when you visit the historical sites in Philadelphia and other places prominent in our colonial society. The chair shown is a replica of such chairs.

When comparing Windsor chairs, it becomes clear that there is no standard angle for the legs in reference to the seat. However, on a single chair it is important that the angle of the front legs match, as is also the case for the rear legs, but the angle of the front legs does not have to equal that of the rear legs. In fact, in most cases the angle of the rear legs and front legs do not match. To obtain the angle of the legs, the chairmakers of the eighteenth century would bore at what was considered a good angle, and place the leg in place. Then by judging how the first leg slanted, the chairmaker would hold his brace and bit as near as possible to the angle of the first leg and bore the second hole. To avoid total guesswork, I use a boring block to support the bit when boring the holes in the seat stock. As can be seen in Figure 6-1, points have been located on the top surface of the seat. These are the entry points for the bits that will bore the $\frac{5}{8}$-in. holes to receive the legs. Also notice that a line drawn from the corner of the stock extends through each entry point. These are the reference lines to align the boring blocks. With the boring block centered on the reference line and positioned so that when the drill bit is placed down through the boring block the bit will contact the seat at the point of entry, the proper compound angle for the legs will be bored. I used an electric hand drill with variable-speed capability. In Figure 6-2 a detail drawing is given for the boring block. You will need three such block. Each block will have a centerline.

Figure 6-3 illustrates the blocks needed to ensure the correct angle for the holes that are to be bored in the legs to receive the side stretchers. These holes should be bored in the leg stock before the stock has been turned. If the leg stock is placed on the proper block and positioned on the table of a drill press, the vertical thrust of the bit in the press will drill the hole to the correct angle. Each piece of stock should be marked as a front leg or rear leg. Otherwise, it will be very easy to place a leg in the incorrect position. If this is done, the chair will not go together.

Figure 6-4 provides the shape of the back. Ideally, this piece should be steamed and bent. If you do not wish to bend the stock, select a piece of stock that has a large knot, as illustrated in Figure 6-4. So doing will provide a natural bending of the grain and thus reduce somewhat the danger of the back piece splitting. The profile of the back is shown in Figure 6-9.

When chiseling out the shape of the seat, you will find it difficult to get all of the seats the same. This is part of the charm of these chairs. Although you will have a set, they will not be exactly the same.

Bill of Materials

Number required	Part name and number	Size (in.)		
		T ×	W ×	L
1	Seat (1)	1	8½	8½
4	Leg (2)	1	1	9½
2	Side stretcher (3)	⅞	⅞	9
1	Center stretcher (4)	⅞	⅞	9
2	Back post (5)	⅞	⅞	10½
1	Back (6)	1½	2¾	11
5	Spindle (7)	½	½	10

STEPS OF PROCEDURE

Note: The dimensions on the drawing were taken from the chair shown in the photograph. Since the slightest difference in the angle at which you drill the holes in the seat will cause significant difference in other dimensions, I recommend that you check all measurements as you proceed. This is the reason that extra length is suggested for the stock or the legs and stretchers. This is noted in Figures 6-5, 6-6, and 6-7.

1. Select the stock for the seat and cut to size.
2. Lay out the angle lines and dimensions as shown in Figure 6-1.
3. Using scrap stock, make three boring guide blocks as shown in Figure 6-2.
4. Bore a ⅝-in. hole on the centerline as shown at an angle of 110 degrees, and mark this block "front legs."
5. Bore a ⅝-in. hole on the centerline of a second block at a 100-degree angle, and mark this block "rear legs."
6. Bore a ½-in. hole on the centerline of the third block at a 75-degree angle, and mark this block "back post."
7. When using the boring blocks, align the centerline on the block with the reference lines on the seat stock, and position the block

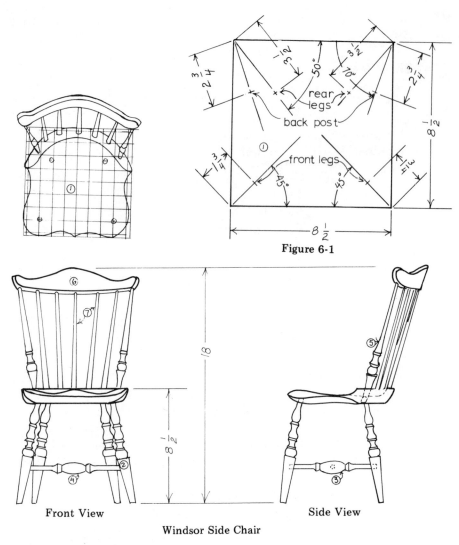

Figure 6-1

Front View   Side View

Windsor Side Chair

Figure 6-2

so that the bit will contact the stock at the entry points laid out on the stock for the seat.

8. With the correct block clamped in place, bore the hole for the right front leg, and then reposition the block to bore the hole for the left front leg.

9. With the correct block clamped in place, bore the hole for the right rear leg, and then reposition the block to bore the hole for the left rear leg.

10. Repeat the process to bore the holes for the back post.

11. Select the stock for the legs, and cut to the correct size.

12. From scrap stock, construct the two blocks shown in Figure 6-3, and mark them as rear leg or front leg, as indicated.

13. With the stock for the front legs positioned on the boring block for the front leg, bore a perpendicular ½-in. hole ⅝-in. deep at a point 3 in. from the bottom end of the leg. See Figure 6-5. Ideally, this should be done on a drill press.

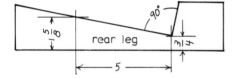

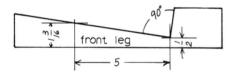

Figure 6-3 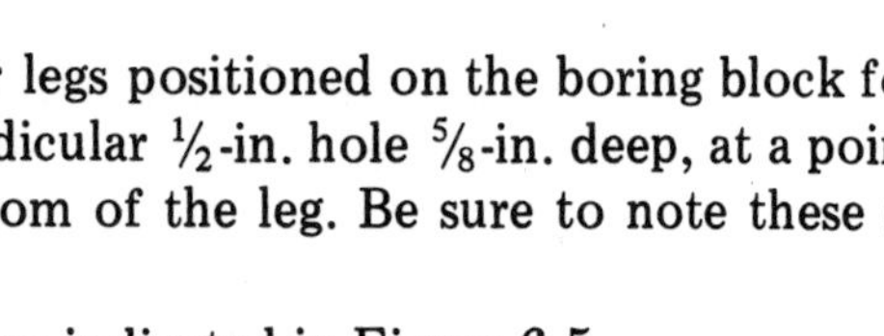   Figure 6-4

14. With the stock for the rear legs positioned on the boring block for the rear legs, bore a perpendicular ½-in. hole ⅝-in. deep, at a point that is 3 in. from the bottom of the leg. Be sure to note these as rear legs.

15. Turn the design on the legs as indicated in Figure 6-5.

16. Place the legs in the proper holes drilled in the seat.

17. Work the legs up through the seat until the seat is 8 in. above the floor and level. See Figure 6-5.

18. Align the legs so that the holes for the stretcher face front to back.

19. At the level of the ½-in. holes on the legs, measure the distance from the front leg to the rear leg.

20. Select the stock for the side stretcher and turn the design as shown in Figure 6-6, leaving the center portion of the design unturned for the time being.

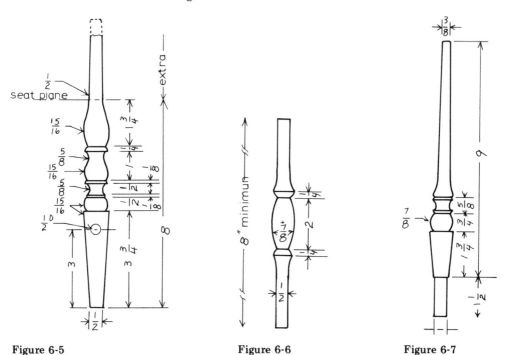

Figure 6-5   Figure 6-6   Figure 6-7

21. Fit the side stretchers to the legs, and mark the center point.

22. By sighting, determine the angle needed for drilling the ½-in. holes at the center point of the side stretchers to accept the center stretcher.

23. Remove the side stretchers from the legs, and bore ½-in. holes in the side stretchers to receive the center stretcher.

24. Complete the turning of the side stretchers.

25. Select the stock for the center stretcher and turn the design as shown in Figure 6-6.

26. With the legs and side stretchers positioned properly, measure the exact distance between the side stretchers, and cutting from both ends of the center stretcher, remove any excess length.

27. The seat and undercarriage of the chair may now be trial-fitted.

28. Select the stock for the back, cut to form as shown in Figure 6-4, and cut the profile as shown in Figure 6-9.

29. Select the stock for the back post and turn to the design shown in Figure 6-7.

30. Place the back post in the proper position in the seat stock.

31. Holding the stock for the back in place, mark the position for the holes to receive the top end of the back post.

32. Once the positions for the holes for the back post have been located, bore $\frac{3}{8}$-in. holes 1 in. deep as illustrated in Figure 6-4.

33. Evenly space positions for five $\frac{3}{8}$-in. holes along the bottom edge of the top and the top surface of the seat to receive the spindles. See Figure 6-4, and the top view.

34. Select the stock for the five back spindles, and turn as shown in Figure 6-8.

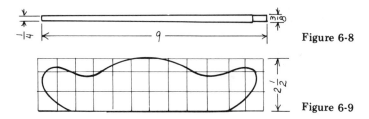

Figure 6-8

Figure 6-9

35. Trial-assemble the entire chair.

36. Disassemble the chair and free-form the seat as shown in the front, side, and top views.

37. For final assembly: using glue, place the legs in the seat and put the stretchers in place.

38. With the chair on a level surface, adjust the seat to be 8 in. from the floor, and level.

39. With a band clamp around the legs at the level of the stretchers, draw the undercarriage to a tight fit.

40. Cut any extra length on the legs that may be protruding above the seating surface.

41. With a $\frac{5}{8}$-in. chisel, start a split in the top of the legs that runs across the grain in the wood for the seat.

42. Drive a $\frac{5}{8}$-in. wedge down into the end grain of the leg to provide a very tight fit.

43. Once the glue is set, sand the seat to your satisfaction, being sure that the top ends of the legs are flush with the seat surface.

44. Glue the back post and spindles in the holes provided in the seat.

45. Glue the top in place by inserting the top ends of the back post and spindles in the holes provided in the top.

46. Gently tap the top down onto the back post and spindles and allow the glue to dry.

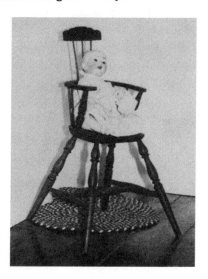

Plate 22   Windsor high chair. Doll: 12-in. German baby.

WINDSOR HIGH CHAIR

The baby sitting in the high chair is quite safe from tipping over, due to the wide splay of the legs. The comb back supports the baby's head and helps to keep the baby in place.

In constructing this chair, allow extra length on the legs, spindles, and arm post. You will find that the slightest difference in the compound angles will create a significant difference in the length of other parts of the chair. Also, when boring the holes for the spindles, a certain amount of individual boring of the holes in the arm will be necessary. Construction of a chair of this type is as much an art as it is craftsmanship. This is what gives these chairs such beauty. When hollowing out the seat to form the profile, do not hesitate to cut rather deep. This will give the chair much character.

Figure 6-17 shows the pattern for one-half of the arm for the chair. Make a full-size pattern of the arm. Select two pieces of stock as given in the bill of materials, and cut an angle as shown in Figure 6-17. Cut two notches so that there will be parallel surfaces for the clamps that will be used to hold the two members of the arm assembly in place when gluing. The spline joint will also provide much needed strength. After the two pieces have been glued, the pattern may be cut.

Although I show the use of boring blocks for boring the holes in the seat, a boring guide can be obtained from the Woodcraft Supply Corporation. The complete address of the company is given in the Introduction.

Bill of Materials

Number required	Part name and number	Size (in.)		
		T ×	W ×	L
4	Leg (1)	$1\frac{1}{4}$	$1\frac{1}{4}$	13
1	Seat (2)	1	8	8
2	Side stretch (3)	1	1	10
1	Center stretch (4)	1	1	$9\frac{1}{2}$
2	Arm post (5)	1	1	$6\frac{1}{2}$
1	Arm (6)	$\frac{1}{2}$	$3\frac{1}{2}$	10
4	Arm spindle (7)	$\frac{1}{4}$	$\frac{1}{4}$	5
3	Back spindle (8)	$\frac{1}{4}$	$\frac{1}{4}$	10
1	Crown (9)	1	$1\frac{3}{4}$	6

STEPS OF PROCEDURE

1. Make a boring guide block, as shown in Figure 6-10, to be used when boring the holes in the seat for the legs and arm post.
2. Making a boring block by drilling a ½-in. hole in the block on the angle shown in Figure 6-11, to be used to bore the holes in the legs for the stretchers.

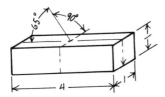

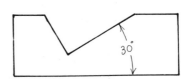

Figure 6-10   Figure 6-11

3. Select the stock for the seat, and cut to size.

4. Lay out the entry points and reference lines as illustrated in Figure 6-12.

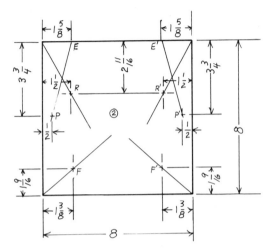

Figure 6-12

5. Align the centerline on the boring block with the reference line F′ for the left front leg, position the block so that the bit will contact the seat at the entry point, and secure with a clamp.

6. Bore a ½-in. hole for the left front leg.

7. Repeat the foregoing process for each leg hole, referencing on lines F, R, and R′.

8. Repeat the steps above for the arm post referencing on reference lines P and P′. Be sure to notice the direction of the slope.

9. Lay out the pattern for the seat as shown in the top view, and cut.

10. Shape the profile of the seat as shown in the side and front views.

11. Bore the ¼-in. holes in the rim of the seat to receive the seven spindles. See the top view.

12. Select the stock for the legs, and cut to the correct size.

13. With the boring block for the legs positioned on the table of a drill, bore a ½-in. hole on center and 5 in. from the bottom end. See Figure 6-13.

14. Turn the design on the legs as shown in Figure 6-13.

15. Trial-fit the legs into the holes in the seat.

16. Select the stock for the side stretchers, and cut to the correct size.

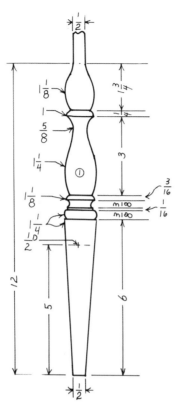

Figure 6-13

17. Place in a lathe, and turn both ends down to ½-in. diameter, leaving a section in the center unturned.

18. Assemble the seat, legs, and side stretchers.

19. Mark the center point on the side stretchers, and determine the angle needed for the ½-in. holes that are to be bored in the side stretchers to receive the center stretcher.

20. Remove the side stretchers from the legs, and bore the ½-in. holes on center.

21. Return the side stretchers to the lathe, and complete turning the design on the side stretchers as shown in the side view.

22. Select the stock for the center stretcher, and turn to the pattern shown in Figure 6-14.

23. With the legs, seat, and side stretchers properly positioned, determine the needed length for the center stretcher, and remove equal amounts from each end, if needed.

24. Select the stock for the arm post, and turn as shown in Figure 6-15.

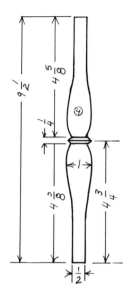

Figure 6-14

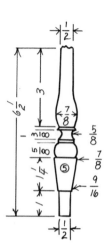

Figure 6-15

25. Select the stock for the arm, and cut the joining angle, clamp
    notches, and the ¼-in.-thick spline as shown in Figure 17. (Refer
    to the discussion in the Introduction concerning construction of
    the arm.)

26. Lay out the arm pattern on the assembled stock, and cut.

27. With the arm post positioned in the seat, hold the arm in place and
    mark the entry point for the post.

28. Drill ½-in. holes through the arm post at the same angle that the
    posts are set in the seat.

29. Mark the position on the arm for the ¼-in. holes that are to receive
    the spindles. See the top view.

30. Place the arm on the post and secure in a level position.

31. By sighting, bore the ¼-in. holes in the arms at an angle that will
    carry to the corresponding holes in the seat.

32. Select the stock for the spindles, and turn.

33. Assemble the seat, arms, and spindles.

34. Select the stock for the crown, and cut to the correct size and
    shape, as shown in Figure 6-16.

35. Hold the crown in the proper position, and mark where the holes
    for the long spindles are to be placed.

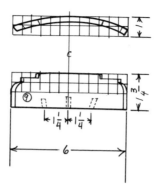

Figure 6-16

36. Bore the three ¼-in. holes in the bottom edge of the crown. (The two outside holes will be at an angle, as indicated in Figure 6-16.)

37. Permanently assemble the seat and undercarriage, making sure that the chair is setting level.

38. After the glue has set, remove any extra leg length that is protruding above the seat of the chair, and sand to your satisfaction.

39. Permanently secure the back, arms, and spindles.

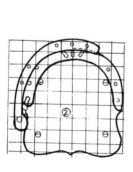

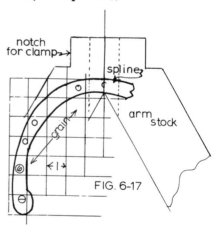

notch for clamp

spline

arm stock

grain

FIG. 6-17

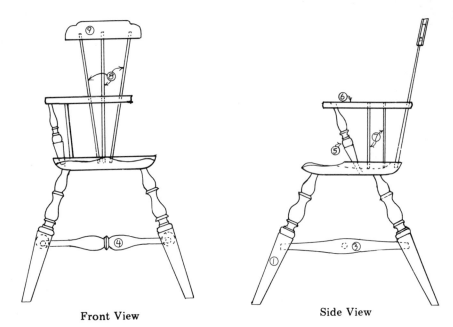

Front View   Side View

Windsor High Chair

Chapter 7

Desk

SLOPE-TOP DESK

W hether it is a student doing studies, or just a place to keep the household accounts, the slope-top desk is a beautiful and very practical piece of furniture. The desk shown is made of walnut. The fine 1½-in. brass drop pulls used to open the drawers were obtained through the Ball and Ball Company, whose address is given in the Introduction.

Bill of Materials

Number required	Part name and number	Size (in.)		
		T ×	W ×	L
2	End (1)	½	10	17½
3	Divider (2)	½	9¾	16½
1	Writing surface (2a)	½	9¾	16½
1	Top (3)	½	4⅝	16½
1	Bottom (4)	½	9¾	16½
1	Lid (5)	½	7¼	16½
4	Feet (6)	1¼	1¼	3
1	False drawer front (7)	½	1⅜	15¼
2	Lid support (8)	⅜	1⅜	9¾
1	Drawer front (9)	½	2¼	16⅛
2	Drawer front (10)	½	3¼	16⅛
2	Drawer side	⅜	2¼	9⅝
4	Drawer side	⅜	3¼	9⅝
1	Drawer back	⅜	1¾	16⅛
2	Drawer back	⅜	2¾	16⅛
3	Drawer bottom	¼	9¼	15¾

1	Back	¼	17¼	16½
1	Molding stock	½	½	40
1	Pigeonhole section (see drawings)			

STEPS OF PROCEDURE

1. Select the stock for the ends, and cut to the correct size.
2. Lay out the position for the stop dado joints as shown in Figure 7-1. The joints are to be ¼-in. deep and ½-in. wide. Be sure to lay out for a left and a right end.
3. Cut the joints in the end stock.
4. Lay out and cut the slope on the end stock as shown in Figure 7-1.

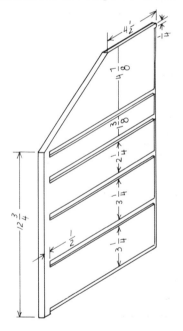

Figure 7-1

5. Select the stock for the dividers, the bottom, and the writing surface, and cut to the correct size.
6. Cut the ¼-in. by ½-in. notch on the front corners of the dividers, the bottom, and the writing surface, as shown in Figure 7-2. The drawer dividers may be made of pine, with a strip of the primary wood glued on the front edge where it can be seen.

7. On the top divider glue a ½-in. by ½-in. by 9-in.-long block to serve as a guide for the lid support. See Figure 7-2.

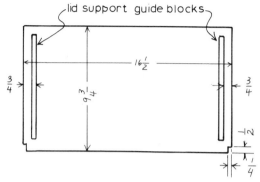

Figure 7-2

8. Trial-assemble the carcass of the desk.

9. Select the stock for the top, and cut to the correct size.

10. Cut the dovetails in the top as shown in Figure 7-3.

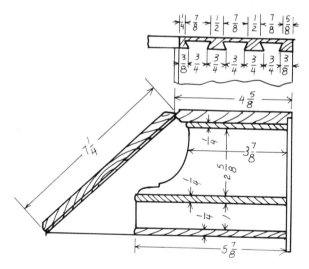

Figure 7-3

11. With the carcass clamped in the correct position, place the top in its proper location, and scribe the outline of the dovetails onto the end grain of the end stock.

12. Disassemble the carcass, and cut the mortises in the end stock to receive the dovetails. *Note:* To avoid splitting the end stock while cutting the mortises, clamp a support block along the outside face of the end stock while doing the work.

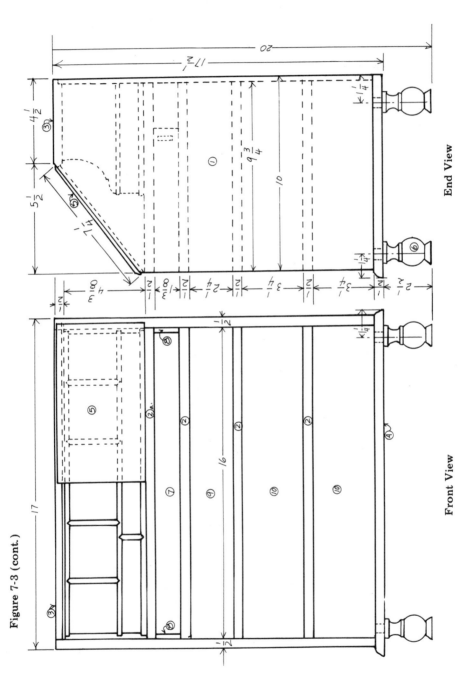

Figure 7-3 (cont.)

End View

Front View

Slope Top Desk

13. Cut a ¼-in. by ¼-in. rabbet on the inside rear corner of each end stock to receive the back. See Figure 7-1.

14. Cut a ¼-in. by ¼-in. rabbet on the inside rear corner of the top.

15. Bore ½-in. holes in the bottom for the feet.

16. Permanently assemble the carcass of the desk.

17. Select the stock for the back, and attach to the carcass using small-headed nails.

18. Select the stock for the lid supports, and cut to the correct size.

19. Glue a stop block on the inside surface of the lid supports 6¾ in. from the front end.

20. Place the lid supports in place.

21. Place the false drawer front in place, and secure with glue.

22. Select the stock for the lid, and cut to the correct size.

23. Cut a ¼-in. by ¼-in. rabbet on the inside corner of the ends and across the top edge of the top.

24. Plane a ⅛-in. by ⅛-in. chamfer around the outside edge of the lid.

25. The lid can be attached with 1-in. brass butt hinges.

26. Select the stock for the drawer fronts, and cut to fit the respective openings. Each front should have approximately ¹⁄₃₂-in. space around the front.

27. Select the drawer sides and backs, and construct the drawers using either the dovetail method or the dado method.

28. Select the bottoms for the drawers and fit in place.

29. Select the stock for the feet, and turn as shown in Figure 7-5.

30. The pigeonhole section should be constructed to the individual builder's own taste. Figures 7-3 and 7-4 provide measurements for the one used in the desk.

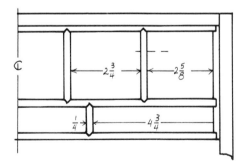

Figure 7-4

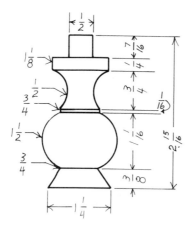

Figure 7-5

31. Secure the stock for the mold to go around the bottom, and shape as shown in Figure 7-6.
32. Fit the molding to the desk using miter joints at the front corners.
33. Attach the molding with small-headed wire brads.

Figure 7-6

Chapter 8

Kitchen Things

Before running water was common in the home, the dry sink served as a place where vegetables and other foods could be cleaned and prepared for cooking. The woman shown seems to be using her potato masher to prepare food.

Bill of Materials

Number required	Part name and number	Size (in.)				
		T	X	W	X	L
2	End (1)	$\frac{1}{2}$		$8\frac{1}{2}$		$19\frac{1}{2}$
1	Tray (8)	$\frac{1}{2}$		8		$16\frac{1}{2}$
1	Bottom (3)	$\frac{1}{2}$		8		$16\frac{1}{2}$
1	Splash back (4)	$\frac{1}{2}$		$6\frac{1}{4}$		$16\frac{1}{2}$
1	Splash front (5)	$\frac{1}{2}$		$1\frac{3}{4}$		17
2	Stile (6)	$\frac{1}{2}$		1		$13\frac{1}{4}$
1	Apron (7)	$\frac{1}{2}$		$2\frac{3}{4}$		16
1	Top (2)	$\frac{1}{2}$		$3\frac{1}{2}$		18
2	Door (9)	$\frac{1}{2}$		$7\frac{1}{2}$		$10\frac{1}{2}$
4	Batten (10)	$\frac{1}{2}$		1		$5\frac{1}{2}$
	Back stock	$\frac{1}{2}$		random		11

STEPS OF PROCEDURE

1. Select the stock for the ends, and cut to the proper size.
2. Locate the position for the dado joints to receive the top and bottom, and mark out using a square and pencil. Be sure to mark for a

left end and a right end. The locations for these dado joints are shown in the end view.

3. On the inside, rear corners of the ends, lay out a ¼-in. by ½-in. rabbet joint to receive the stock for the back.

4. Cut the dado joints and the rabbet joints in the end stock.

5. Lay out the design for the feet on the ends, and cut.

6. Lay out the design for the step-back on the end stock, and cut.

7. Select the stock for the bottom and the tray, and cut to the correct size.

8. Temporarily assemble the ends, tray, and bottom, in the position that will eventually be the permanent position.

9. Select the stock for the front splash board, and cut to the proper width and length so that the board will terminate flush with the outside surface of the ends.

10. Select the stock for the rear splash board, and cut to the correct width.

11. Cut the length that will allow the rear splash board to fit snug between the shoulders of the rabbet joint that has been cut in the inside corners of the end stock.

12. Select the stock for the stiles, and cut to the correct size.

13. Select the stock for the apron, and cut to the correct size.

14. Assemble the stiles and apron with mortise-and-tenon joints as illustrated in Figure 8-1.

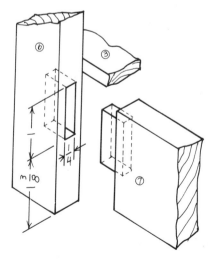

Figure 8-1

15. Trial-fit the apron and stile assembly to the front of the dry sink.

16. Remove the apron and stile assembly, and cut the design on the apron as shown in the front view.

17. All of the pieces that have been prepared thus far may be permanently assembled, using glue and small-headed nails.

18. Select the stock for the top, and cut to the correct size.

19. The top may be attached to the sink by driving nails down through the shelf into the end grain of the ends.

20. Select the stock for the doors, and cut to the correct size.

21. Select stock for the battens, and cut to the correct size.

22. Fasten the battens to the inside face of the doors as shown in Figure 8-2.

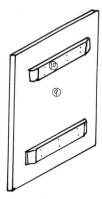

Figure 8-2

23. The doors may be fastened with flush-mounted butt hinges.

24. Select the stock for the back of the cabinet.

25. Cut the stock to the correct length.

26. Cut alternating half-lap joints in the edges of the back stock as shown in Figure 8-3, and attach the back using small-headed nails or brads.

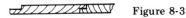 Figure 8-3

27. The doors should have turnbuckles for keepers. Refer to Chapter 1 for details on making turnbuckles.

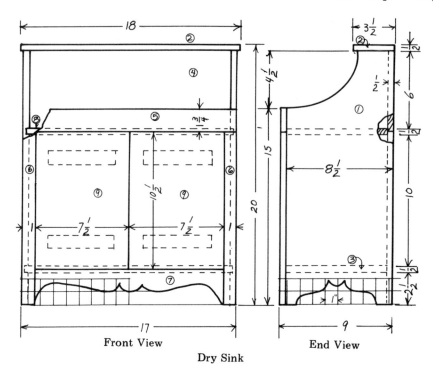

Front View   End View

Dry Sink

BUCKET BENCH

The bucket bench was used as a place to put buckets of water so that
they would be readily available when workers returned from the field.
It was here that workers would wash their faces and hands. The young
worker shown here has just come to the house for food and rest, and is
washing off the dust of his labors.

Plate 25   Bucket bench. Doll: 20-in.
Shoenhut wood boy.

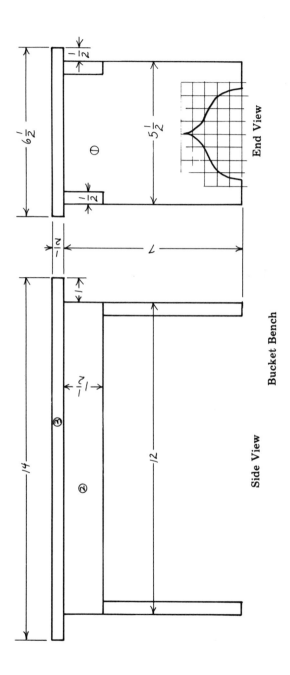

Bucket Bench

End View

Side View

Bill of Materials

Number required	Name of part and number	Size (in.)		
		T X	W X	L
2	Leg (1)	½	5½	7
2	Brace (2)	½	1½	12
1	Top (3)	½	6½	14

STEPS OF PROCEDURE

1. Select the stock for the legs, and cut to correct size.
2. Lay out the design for the feet, and cut accordingly.
3. Cut the ½-in. by 1½-in. notch in the upper corners of the legs for the braces.
4. Select the stock for the braces, and cut to size.
5. Secure the braces to the legs, using glue and nails.
6. Select the stock for the top, and cut to size.
7. Secure the top to the braces either by gluing the top to the top edges of the braces or with small-headed nails driven down through the top into the braces.

Chapter 9

Accessories

CANDLE HOLDER

The candle was the main source for light in the colonial household, and many types of holders were developed to make the most use of the light provided. The holder being used by this woman has a threaded pedestal which allows for the lowering or raising of the candle. The tray under the candle protects the floor from wax drippings.

A ½-in.-diameter wood die and tap will be needed to make the candle holder. Threaders can be obtained from the Woodcraft Supply Corporation. The complete address of the company is listed in the Introduction.

Bill of Materials

Number required	Part name and number	Size (in.)				
		T	X	W	X	L
1	Pedestal (1)	1		1		14⅜
1	Base (2)	⅞		3		3
1	Tray (3)	½		7		7
1	Arm (4)	⅞		⅞		8
3	Leg (5)	⅝		⅝		6¼

STEPS OF PROCEDURE

1. Select the stock for the pedestal and turn the design shown.
2. Using a ½-in. threading tool, turn a thread over the ⅝-in.-diameter section of the pedestal.

3. Select the stock for the base and turn to a 3-in.-diameter, being sure to turn a 30-degree chamfer on the lower edge.

4. Bore a ⅝-in. hole through the center of the base to receive the dowel turned on the bottom of the pedestal.

5. Bore three ⅜-in. holes 120 degrees apart on the chamfered portion of the base, and on an angle of 90 degrees to the chamfered portion.

6. Select the stock for the legs, and turn as shown in Figure 9-1.

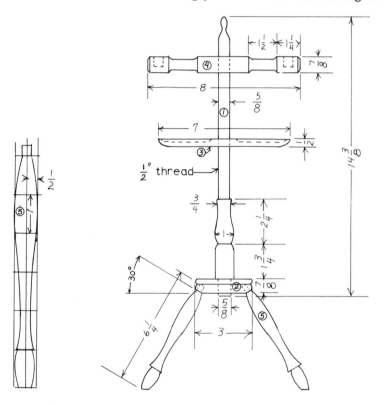

Figure 9-1　　　　　　　　　　　Candle Holder

7. Fit the legs to the base.

8. Select the stock for the tray, and turn a concaved surface as the dashed lines indicate in the main view.

9. Bore a ½-in. hole through the center of the tray.

10. Using a ½-in. tap, thread the hole in the tray.

11. Select the stock for the arm, bore a ½-in. hole through the stock at the center, and bore two ⅜-in. holes ⅝-in. deep at a point that is ⅝ in. from the ends.
12. Turn the design on the arm stock as shown in the main view.
13. Permanently fit the legs to the base, using glue.
14. Permanently fit the pedestal to the base, using glue.

COOKING UTENSILS

The potato masher and the rolling pin are two of the most common tools in the kitchen. They should be made of maple or other tight-grained light-colored wood.

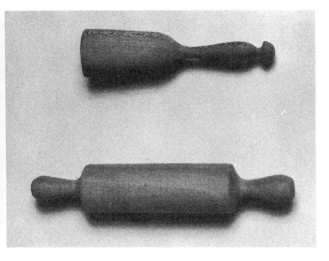

Plate 27   Rolling pin/potato masher.

Bill of Material

		Size (in.)		
		T ×	W ×	L
Rolling pin		1½	1½	7
1	Body stock			
Potato masher				
1	Body stock	1¼	1¼	5¼

STEPS OF PROCEDURE

1. For either piece (Figure 9-2) select the stock, and cut it to the correct width and thickness.

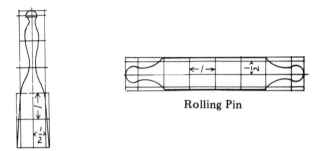

Rolling Pin

Potato Masher   Figure 9-2

2. Cut the length about ¾-in. too long.
3. Turn the stock to the appropriate shape, leaving about ⅜-in. waste stock on both ends.
4. Remove the work from the lathe, and smooth the ends by hand.